Online

Congratulations! You now have access to practical templates of the Data Analytics concepts that you will learn in this book. Data analytics often involves the use of structured data tables to organize information in a way that's conducive to more efficient analysis. Here are the titles of ten table templates that will help you organize data for efficient analysis.

They are:

- Data Quality Assessment Table
- User Demographic Analysis Table
- Sales Performance Analysis Table
- Website Traffic Analysis Table
- Customer Feedback Analysis Table
- Inventory Management Analysis Table
- Marketing Campaign Analysis Table
- Financial Transaction Analysis Table
- Product Quality Analysis Table
- Employee Performance Analysis Table
- Additional videos and articles for reference

To access the templates, follow the steps below:

1. Go to www.vibrantpublishers.com
2. Click on the 'Online Resources' option on the Home Page
3. Login by entering your account details (or create an account if you don't have one)
4. Go to the Self-Learning Management series section on the Online Resources page
5. Click the 'Data Analytics Essentials You Always Wanted To Know' link and access the templates.

More information on how to use the templates

Each of these tables is designed to gather and organize data critical for analytics in various domains, allowing for efficient querying, reporting, and decision-making processes in organizations. In other words, the tables help the users make the first steps in data analytics. The templates can be used in a variety of industries and for a variety of purposes. Here is more information on how to use them.

- **Data Quality Assessment:** The Data Quality Assessment Table can be used to assess the quality of a dataset by identifying and correcting errors, inconsistencies, and missing values. This is an important step in any data analysis project, as it ensures that the results are accurate and reliable.

- **User Demographic Analysis:** The User Demographic Analysis Table can be used to analyze the demographic characteristics of a user base, such as age, gender, location, and occupation. This information can be used to better understand user needs and preferences, and to develop more targeted marketing and product development strategies.

- **Sales Performance Analysis:** The Sales Performance Analysis Table can be used to analyze sales data over time to identify which type of products are most often sold, which products are more profitable, or in what sales region the company has the most sales. This information can be used to set sales goals, develop sales strategies, and motivate sales teams.

- **Website Traffic Analysis:** The Website Traffic Analysis Table can be used to analyze website traffic data to identify popular pages, visitor sources, and visitor behavior. This information can be used to improve the user experience, optimize marketing campaigns, and increase website conversions.

- **Customer Feedback Analysis:** The Customer Feedback Analysis Table can be used to analyze customer feedback data to identify areas for improvement and develop new products and services. This information can also be used to track customer satisfaction levels over time.

- **Inventory Management Analysis:** The Inventory Management Analysis Table can be used to track inventory levels, identify trends in demand, and optimize inventory levels. This information can help businesses to avoid stockouts and overstocking and to improve their bottom line.

- **Marketing Campaign Analysis:** The Marketing Campaign Analysis Table can be used to track the results of marketing campaigns and identify which campaigns are most effective. This information can be used to optimize marketing budgets and improve campaign ROI.

- **Financial Transaction Analysis:** The Financial Transaction Analysis Table can be used to track and analyze financial transactions to identify trends, patterns, and potential fraud. This information can be used to improve financial management and make better financial decisions.

- **Product Quality Analysis:** The Product Quality Analysis Table can be used to track and analyze product quality data to identify areas for improvement. This information can be used to improve product design, manufacturing processes, and quality control procedures.

- **Employee Performance Analysis:** The Employee Performance Analysis Table can be used to track and analyze employee performance data to identify top performers, areas for improvement, and training needs. This information can be used to develop performance management plans, reward high-performing employees, and improve employee engagement.

Overall, the downloadable 10 Excel templates related to the data analytics field are a valuable resource for anyone who wants to use data to improve their work. The templates are easy to use and can be customized to meet the specific needs of each user.

Here are some specific examples of how the templates can be used in different industries:

- **E-commerce:** The User Demographic Analysis Table can be used to identify the target market for an e-commerce company. The Sales Performance Analysis Table can be used to track sales data over time and identify trends. The Website Traffic Analysis Table can be used to identify popular products and pages.

- **Retail:** The Inventory Management Analysis Table can be used to track inventory levels and avoid stockouts. The Marketing Campaign Analysis Table can be used to track the results of marketing campaigns and identify which campaigns are most effective. The Customer Feedback Analysis Table can be used to identify areas for improvement and develop new products and services.

- **Manufacturing:** The Product Quality Analysis Table can be used to track and analyze product quality data to identify areas for improvement. The Financial Transaction Analysis Table can be used to track and analyze financial transactions to identify trends, patterns, and potential fraud.

Happy self-learning!

SELF-LEARNING MANAGEMENT SERIES

VIBRANT
PUBLISHERS

DATA ANALYTICS ESSENTIALS

YOU ALWAYS WANTED TO KNOW

From raw data to actionable insights - journey through the essentials of data analytics.

BIANCA SZASZ

Data Analytics Essentials You Always Wanted To Know

First Edition

Paperback ISBN 10: 1-63651-118-X
Paperback ISBN 13: 978-1-63651-118-4

Ebook ISBN 10: 1-63651-119-8
Ebook ISBN 13: 978-1-63651-119-1

Hardback ISBN 10: 1-63651-120-1
Hardback ISBN 13: 978-1-63651-120-7

Library of Congress Control Number: 2022938403

This publication is designed to provide accurate and authoritative information in regard to the subject matter covered. The Author has made every effort in the preparation of this book to ensure the accuracy of the information. However, information in this book is sold without warranty either expressed or implied. The Author or the Publisher will not be liable for any damages caused or alleged to be caused either directly or indirectly by this book.

Vibrant Publishers books are available at special quantity discount for sales promotions, or for use in corporate training programs. For more information please write to bulkorders@vibrantpublishers.com

Please email feedback / corrections (technical, grammatical or spelling) to spellerrors@vibrantpublishers.com

To access the complete catalogue of Vibrant Publishers, visit www.vibrantpublishers.com

SELF-LEARNING MANAGEMENT SERIES

TITLE	PAPERBACK* ISBN

ACCOUNTING, FINANCE & ECONOMICS

COST ACCOUNTING AND MANAGEMENT ESSENTIALS	9781636511030
FINANCIAL ACCOUNTING ESSENTIALS	9781636510972
FINANCIAL MANAGEMENT ESSENTIALS	9781636511009
MACROECONOMICS ESSENTIALS	9781636511818
MICROECONOMICS ESSENTIALS	9781636511153
PERSONAL FINANCE ESSENTIALS	9781636511849

ENTREPRENEURSHIP & STRATEGY

BUSINESS PLAN ESSENTIALS	9781636511214
BUSINESS STRATEGY ESSENTIALS	9781949395778
ENTREPRENEURSHIP ESSENTIALS	9781636511603

GENERAL MANAGEMENT

BUSINESS LAW ESSENTIALS	9781636511702
DATA ANALYTICS ESSENTIALS	9781636511184
DECISION MAKING ESSENTIALS	9781636510026
LEADERSHIP ESSENTIALS	9781636510316
PRINCIPLES OF MANAGEMENT ESSENTIALS	9781636511542
TIME MANAGEMENT ESSENTIALS	9781636511665

*Also available in Hardback & Ebook formats

SELF-LEARNING MANAGEMENT SERIES

TITLE	PAPERBACK* ISBN
HUMAN RESOURCE MANAGEMENT	
DIVERSITY IN THE WORKPLACE ESSENTIALS	9781636511122
HR ANALYTICS ESSENTIALS	9781636510347
HUMAN RESOURCE MANAGEMENT ESSENTIALS	9781949395839
ORGANIZATIONAL BEHAVIOR ESSENTIALS	9781636510378
ORGANIZATIONAL DEVELOPMENT ESSENTIALS	9781636511481

MARKETING & SALES MANAGEMENT	
DIGITAL MARKETING ESSENTIALS	9781949395747
MARKETING MANAGEMENT ESSENTIALS	9781636511788
SALES MANAGEMENT ESSENTIALS	9781636510743
SERVICES MARKETING ESSENTIALS	9781636511733
SOCIAL MEDIA MARKETING ESSENTIALS	9781636512181

OPERATIONS & PROJECT MANAGEMENT	
AGILE ESSENTIALS	9781636510057
OPERATIONS & SUPPLY CHAIN MANAGEMENT ESSENTIALS	9781949395242
PROJECT MANAGEMENT ESSENTIALS	9781636510712
STAKEHOLDER ENGAGEMENT ESSENTIALS	9781636511511

*Also available in Hardback & Ebook formats

About the Author

 Bianca Szasz is a Romanian with a Ph.D. in Space Engineering from Japan. With over 14 years of experience in engineering and a dedicated focus of 4 years on data analytics, her journey is proof of the transformative potential of data.

She played a pivotal role in the Shinen2 University space mission. Next, she embraced the role of Special Assistant Professor at Nagoya University where she guided graduate students as part of the Leadership Development Program for Space Exploration and Research.

Her book Data Analytics Essentials is the result of both her in-depth knowledge of the subject and her intellectual curiosity. What ignited her interest in data analytics was its potential to transform entire sectors.

She has used data analytics in a variety of innovative projects over her career, notably to perform post-processing of the wind tunnel test results in Germany, and analyzing high enthalpy heating test results during her doctoral research in Japan. Due to these experiences and many others, she was able to see firsthand how data analytics tremendously boosts research and engineering projects. Her passion for data analytics goes beyond applications in the workplace - she has a strong desire to educate those who are unfamiliar with data analytics.

What experts say about this book!

I think this text is a comprehensive yet succinct manual. It gives a usable introduction to data analytics and is easy to read and comprehend. An added benefit is that the book contains real-world case studies and interesting facts to help enhance existing knowledge.

A key strength of this text is the option to choose the topics that you want to focus on and the resources that you want to use. This flexibility makes self-directed learning a great option for busy professionals who want to add data analytics skills to their repertoire. If you're interested in self-directed learning for data analytics, there are a few things you need to do to get started, and this text will help!

**– David E Reva, Instructor - CIS,
Kalamazoo Valley Community College**

The book is written in a way that makes it easier for complete beginners like me to understand the world of data analytics. Every chapter has a helpful summary and a quiz to test your knowledge. Fascinating!

**– Chiara Colombo, Sr Contracts Analyst,
Yahoo! Inc.**

An absolutely valuable book that can help structure your knowledge in data science and data analytics. If you are at an advanced level, the book may not be for you. However if you are looking to shape your experience or are interested in switching careers to data analytics, this book is a great help. It provides an overview of the field, presents a structured knowledge set, and gives a good understanding of the topic.

**– Darya Yegorina, DBA, Chief of Staff Strategy & Sales Ops,
Verizon**

This book is a comprehensive and detailed "map" of Data Analytics, which professionals can use in the initial years of their career. The book covers everything you need to know at the beginning of the journey and will help you make wise decisions such as which software tool to use to solve a specific problem and what are its advantages and disadvantages. The book abounds with practical examples, quizzes, and good practice tips.

– Cătălin Neacşu,
Doctor of Philosophy (Ph.D) in Physics

The book is an excellent resource for anyone interested in data analytics. Whether you're a student, professional, or simply a curious learner, this book provides the knowledge and tools needed to navigate and excel in the world of data analytics.

– Tamer Abu Rouk,
Space Engineer

Great book! It helped me understand all we can do with data analytics tools and, thanks to this book, I have started to implement some data analytics techniques at my own job!

– Sara Szasz,
Chief Economist

This book is excellent as it provides a versatile guide to data analytics for all levels, catering both to beginners as well as for those more experienced in the field. Beginners will appreciate how it simplifies complex concepts, offering clear, structured chapters that make learning the basics both manageable and engaging. For seasoned analysts, the book is a valuable reference, delving into advanced topics with clarity and offering practical, real-world applications of various analytics tools.

– Dana Neacşu,
Competitive Analyst

Table of Contents

Preface

Understanding and utilizing data analytics is becoming a universal need that spans every sector and industry in this revolutionary era of data. It is no longer a specialty but an essential concept that everyone should know about. Data Analytics Essentials was created to meet this exact need. It is designed to be a foundational manual for professionals entering this rapidly evolving industry and students hoping to pursue a career in data analytics. In addition to explaining the essentials of data analytics, this book is also a compass that will guide you through the complexity of data patterns, forecasts, and strategic decision-making in the world of data. It will make you an active participant in the data's evolution rather than just a spectator.

It has been nothing less than an adventure for me to travel from exploring the complexities of space engineering to embracing the wide world of data analytics. Both domains are supported by inquiry, logic, and the never-ending pursuit of knowledge. As a result, I have ensured that this book combines structured approaches with real-world examples to provide a comprehensive introduction to data analytics.

By the end of this book you will be able to answer the following questions regarding concepts in the area of Data Analytics:

- What is Data Analytics, and why is it crucial in the modern business environment?

- What are the primary components and processes in Data Analytics, and how do they contribute to obtaining actionable insights?

- What are the responsibilities and typical decision-making processes for analysts within this domain?

- How do disruptions or innovations in data technology influence business strategies, operations, and everyday life?

- What are the real-world implications and applications of advancements and trends in Data Analytics, including examples of transformative impacts?

To the students, let this book serve as your academic cornerstone, helping you connect theoretical knowledge with the practical skills that your prospective employers will be looking for. If you're a professional about to change or begin your career, think of this as your spark, your stepping-stone towards a bright career. Whether you're entering the world of banking, healthcare, retail, or everything in between, the ideas and procedures covered in these pages offer insightful viewpoints.

As you turn these pages, I encourage you to maintain the spirit of inquiry and critical thinking, important traits in the realm of data analytics. If you embrace the process, you'll learn more about yourself as well as the trends in the data. Welcome to Data Analytics Essentials – where your journey into the heart of data begins!

Bianca Szasz

Acknowledgments

I would like to express my sincere appreciation to the entire team of Vibrant Publishers, whose commitment and exceptional editing skills have been indispensable in shaping and directing the content to our wide readership. I am also very grateful to all those involved in the marketing team, whose creative approaches have helped to make this work much more visible.

I want to thank my family lastly for their endless patience and support, I surely needed it.

Without the combined efforts and encouragement of all of you, this book would not have been possible. I appreciate all that you have done to make our trip successful and memorable.

How to use this book?

We took flexibility into consideration when writing this book, understanding that readers have different backgrounds and aspirations in the field of data analytics. Various readers may approach the text in the following ways:

1. If you're totally new to the field of data analytics, start with Chapter 1 to gain a basic understanding and work your way up to understand the nuances as your knowledge base grows.

2. Chapters 2 and 4 include an abundance of information about the techniques and resources that simplify data processing and management, making them indispensable resources for professionals who concentrate on the practical elements of the field. Chapter 3 is a theoretical elaboration on the four types of data analytics.

3. Chapter 5 provides insights into your future career, duties, and the influence of your work, which will be insightful for you as an aspiring data analyst. This in-depth analysis makes clear what is expected of you in this role and what you can anticipate.

4. Should you have a particular interest in Big Data, you should read Chapter 6. This section explains the idea, explores its major impact, and outlines its applicability across a range of sectors.

5. You should not skip Chapter 7 if you are concerned about the ethical consequences of using data. Anybody who works with data should read it carefully to make sure their work complies with the strictest ethical guidelines and respects privacy restrictions.

6. The case studies in Chapter 8 will be very helpful to practitioners searching for concrete, real-world uses and outcomes of data analytics. These real-world examples highlight the theories and approaches covered in the book.

Allow this book to serve as your guide through the complex world of data analytics by freely navigating through the chapters according to your requirements and interests.

Who can benefit from this book?

Individuals Looking to Switch Careers: Do you have aspirations to mix things up in your work? A career in data analytics can be your ticket to a fulfilling job. With Data Analytics Essentials, you will acquire the ability to integrate analytics with your existing talents, preparing you for careers as a data scientist, business analyst, or data analyst. In addition, a plethora of sectors, like tech, retail, finance, and health, will want you on their team.

Students and recent graduates: This book will support you if you're at a moment in your career search or studies where you need to make important decisions. Data Analytics Essentials gives you a strong foundation by explaining everything in an easy-to-understand language. You will acquire knowledge about skills that are in high demand across numerous sectors. Thus, you're not only acquiring knowledge; you're also making yourself highly desirable to potential employers!

This page is intentionally left blank

Chapter 1

Introduction to Data Analytics

Get ready to embark on a fascinating journey into the realm of data analytics! This introductory chapter unveils what data analytics truly is, sifting through the vast sands of data to uncover invaluable insights, akin to a gold miner. We'll clarify the distinction between data science and data analytics while underlining the significance of data analytics in the modern world. Additionally, a quick overview of this intriguing field's history will be provided, followed by an explanation of its key concepts.

The key learning objectives of this chapter should include the reader's understanding of the following:

- The definition of data analytics
- The difference between data analytics and data science
- The importance of data analytics for modern enterprises

- The key historical milestones of the evolution of data analytics as a field of study

- The key concepts used in data analytics

1.1 What is Data Analytics?

Firstly, you might ask what data analytics really is. In this chapter, we will take a look at the definition of the vast domain of data analytics. Get ready and let's dive into the captivating world of data analytics!

Data is everywhere. Every time you post a comment on social media or upload a file, a picture, a piece of music, or a short video, you contribute to the data increase.[1]

Data analytics, at its core, is about making sense of all this raw information. It is the process of collecting, pre-processing, transforming, modeling, and interpreting data to extract useful knowledge (patterns) from them, draw conclusions, predict future trends, and guide decision-making[2].

While the terms data analysis and data analytics may sometimes be used interchangeably, they aren't identical. While both focus on gleaning insights from data, data analytics places a particular emphasis on the application of those insights to inform

---

1. Moreira, J. M., de Carvalho, A. C. P. L. F., and Horváth, T. 2019. *A General Introduction to Data Analytics*. John Wiley & Sons, Inc.

2. Gudivada, V.N. 2017. *Data Analytics for Intelligent Transportation Systems*. Elsevier, ISBN 978-0-12-809715-1.

better business decisions.[3] Think of data analysis as the detective work, and data analytics as putting those clues into action.

Now, how does this process work? The journey of data analytics often moves through several stages. There is no one specific method for a project on data analytics, but usually, the following steps are involved:

a. Understanding the problem to be solved

b. Defining the objectives of the project

c. Looking for the necessary data

d. Preparing these data so that they can be used

e. Identifying suitable data analysis methods and choosing between them

f. Tuning the hyper-parameters of each method

g. Analyzing and evaluating the results

h. Redoing the preprocessing tasks if necessary and repeating the experiments.[4]

This meticulous process ensures that businesses can make the most out of their data. Roughly, we can consider 5 stages of a data analytics process: **identifying, collecting, cleaning, analyzing, and interpreting data.**

Data analytics isn't just about numbers and algorithms; it is about asking the right questions and making informed decisions.

3. Nanda, P., Kumar, V. 2022. *Information Processing and Data Analytics for Decision Making: A Journey From Traditional to Modern Approaches.* Information Resources Management Journal, Volume 35, Issue 2. DOI: 10.4018/IRMJ.291693.

4. Moreira, J. M., de Carvalho, A. C. P. L. F., and Horváth, T. 2019. *A General Introduction to Data Analytics.* John Wiley & Sons, Inc..

It leverages a variety of tools, from basic ones like spreadsheets to R, Python, RapidMiner, Hadoop, Spark, Tableau, and KNIME to dive deep into data and extract meaningful insights.[5] Each tool plays its unique part in the symphony of data analytics, enabling businesses to interpret complex data and make strategic decisions.

Remember, data analytics isn't a one-time task. It is a cyclical, iterative process that keeps evolving with every new piece of data and insight. It helps us know the world better, enabling us to make better decisions. It is about constantly learning from the past, optimizing the present, and strategizing for the future.

In a nutshell, data analytics is like a compass in the vast ocean of data, guiding businesses toward their goals. So next time you come across a big decision, remember - there's probably data out there to help light your path!

1.2 How is Data Analytics Different From Data Science?

Besides data analytics, another term we often hear is data science. What is the difference between them? Are they the same? Well, both are fascinating fields that deal with data, but they have unique focuses and applications.

Data analytics refers to the process and practice of analyzing data to answer specific questions, extract insights, and identify

5. Bonthu, Sridevi, and K Hima Bindu. 2017. *Review of Leading Data Analytics Tools.* International Journal of Engineering & Technology, 7 (3.31) 10-15.

trends.[6] Think of data analytics as the magnifying glass that zooms in on the data, helping us find answers to particular questions and identify actionable insights. [7]

On the other hand, data science takes a broader view. It includes data analytics as a part, but it also explores unstructured data using advanced tools like machine learning and artificial intelligence. It's not just about finding answers to existing questions, but also about asking new, strategic-level questions and driving innovation.

This difference in scope means that a data scientist's role is typically broader than that of a data analyst.[8] A data scientist may even start their career as a data analyst and then expand their skills and knowledge to include more data science techniques.

6. Stobierski, Tim. 2021. *A Beginner's Guide to Value-based Strategy*. Harvard Business School Online. 5 January. Accessed May 23, 2023. https://online.hbs.edu/blog/post/data-analytics-vs-data-science.

7. Tsyen, N., Chan, T. 2016. *Defining and Conceptualizing Actionable Insight: A Conceptual Framework for Decision-centric Analytics*. Conference Proceedings of the Australasian Conference on Information Systems.

8. Maryville's online Bachelor of Science in *Data Science*. 2023. *Data Science vs. Data Analytics: Understanding the Differences*. Accessed May 22, 2023. https://online.maryville.edu/blog/data-science-vs-data-analytics/.

Fun Fact

Although the term "data science" has been around for some time, in 2008 it took on new significance. The present concept of "data scientist" is credited to D.J. Patil and Jeff Hammerbacher[9]. The most interesting part is that many people frequently refer to the work of a data scientist as "data janitor" work since it requires a lot of data cleaning and organization before any significant discoveries can be made.

Key skills and tools also differ between the two. For instance, while both require programming skills, data science often utilizes machine learning algorithms and data mining activities to extract insights, while data analytics usually does not.

One way to think about the difference is through the types of questions they answer. Descriptive, diagnostic, predictive, and prescriptive analytics are the four types of data analytics, each answering a specific type of question. Data science, meanwhile, may ask broader, more open-ended questions that innovate and explore new possibilities. In fact, data science is one of the most significant advances of the early twenty-first century.[10]

To sum it up, data analytics is like the Sherlock Holmes of data, working with a magnifying glass to answer specific questions and solve defined problems. Data science, on the other hand, is more of a visionary like Galileo, using a telescope to explore the vast

9. Kim, M., Zimmermann, T., DeLine, R., Begel, A. 2016. *The Emerging Role of Data Scientists on Software Development Teams.* Proceedings of The 2016 IEEE/ACM 38th IEEE International Conference on Software Engineering. DOI: http://dx.doi.org/10.1145/2884781.2884783.

10. Brodie, M.L. 2019. *What Is Data Science?* Applied Data Science (pp.101-130). DOI:10.1007/978-3-030-11821-1_8 .

cosmos of data and discover new horizons. And just like Holmes and Galileo, both have a critical role to play in understanding our data-filled world!

1.3 The Importance of Data Analytics in Today's World

Data analytics is integral to business operations, allowing leadership to develop evidence-based strategies, understand customers better, and enhance efficiency. [11]

In our fast-paced digital world, data analytics plays a pivotal role in driving business growth. It provides us with invaluable insights, helping to illuminate the path to success and giving us a competitive edge. Think of it as the headlights of a car in the darkness, helping businesses see the road ahead and avoid obstacles.

Table 1.1 illustrates how firms can benefit greatly from current business challenges by adopting a more analytical and data-driven approach. Any firm faces four main challenges: maximizing operations, identifying risk, forecasting new opportunities, and adhering to legal and regulatory obligations. Stated differently, these are generally referred to as the primary business drivers. These four drivers can be converted into a number of factors that data analytics may employ to study and regulate. For example, to optimize business operations, data analytics can be used to calculate the number of sales, pricing, profitability, and efficiency.

11. University of Pennsylvania. 2022. *5 key reasons why data analytics is important to business.* 20 October. Accessed May 20, 2023. https://lpsonline.sas.upenn.edu/features/5-key-reasons-why-data-analytics-important-business.

In other words, by calculating and controlling sales, pricing, profitability, and efficiency, business operations can be optimized. The same principle can be applied to other examples in Table 1.1. By monitoring customer churn, fraud, and default, the business risk can be identified. By investigating the upsell, cross-sell, and the best new customer prospects, new business opportunities can be predicted. And, by carefully obeying the Anti-Money Laundering, Fair Lending, Basel II-III, Sarbanes-Oxley (SOX) policies, the business can make sure that it complies with the main laws and regulatory requirements. All these tasks require data analytics at its core.

Table 1.1	Business drivers for advanced analytics
Business Driver	**Examples**
Optimize business operations	Sales, pricing, profitability, efficiency
Identify business risk	Customer churn, fraud, default
Predict new business opportunities	Upsell, cross-sell, best new customer prospects
Comply with laws or regulatory requirements	Anti-Money Laundering, Fair Lending, Basel II-III, Sarbanes-Oxley (SOX)

Source: Long, C. et al. 2015. Data Science & Big Data Analytics: Discovering, Analyzing, Visualizing and Presenting Data. John Wiley & Sons, Inc., Canada. ISBN: 978-1-118-87613-8.

One significant aspect where data analytics shines is in its ability to turn consumer feedback into profitable insights. Effective use of data analysis could be the key to transforming a failing product line into a quality one that truly satisfies customers' needs, driving profits and business growth.[12]

Big data is a well-known concept, representing massive data sets with large, diverse, and complicated structures that are challenging to store, analyze, and visualize for additional procedures or outcomes[13] . The rise of big data has also created new challenges and opportunities. Traditional data protection principles are struggling to cope with the complexity and opaqueness of big data analytics. This evolution calls for innovative solutions and underscores the growing importance of data transparency in the realm of data analytics. [14]

As businesses generate and collect massive amounts of data, it is essential to invest in advanced analytics to leverage new and innovative sources of data. Organizations that can pivot swiftly and create new insights from their data are the ones that will thrive in today's business world.[15]

Quick Tips

Although big data gets a lot of attention, often the most useful insights come from smaller data sets.

---

12. Moreira, João Mendes, André C. P. L. F. de Carvalho, and Tomáš Horváth. 2019. *A General Introduction to Data Analytics.* John Wiley & Sons, Inc.

13. Yaseen, H.K., Obaid, A.M. 2020. *Big Data: Definition, Architecture & Applications.* International Journal on Informatics Visualization. Vol.4 (2020), No.1, e-ISSN : 2549-9904, ISSN : 2549-9610.

14. Bormida, Marina Da. 2021. *The Big Data World: Benefits, Threats and Ethical Challenges.* Iphofen, R. and O'Mathúna, D. (Ed.) Ethical Issues in Covert, Security and Surveillance Research (Advances in Research Ethics and Integrity, Vol. 8, Emerald Publishing Limited, Bingley 71-91.

15. Wang, J. 2021. *The Importance of Data Analytics in Today's Business World.* Australian National Institute of Management and Commerce. 23 July. Accessed May 22, 2023. https://www.imc.edu.au/news-archive/the-importance-of-data-analytics-in-today-s-business-world.

In a nutshell, data analytics is the fuel that powers the engine of modern businesses. It's the treasure map that reveals the path to success in the complex labyrinth of data. And in this ever-evolving digital era, the importance of data analytics is only set to increase.

1.4 Brief History of Data Analytics

How have we come so far? How did data analytics emerge as a field of study? The story of data analytics is a thrilling journey of human achievement, steeped in the pursuit of understanding the world through the lens of data.

Our journey starts in ancient times with the first use of data. The history of data goes back to 19,000 BCE when the Palaeolithic ancestors invented the Ishango bone, a tool to perform simple math calculations[16]. This is considered one of the earliest records of human scientific endeavor.

 The financial analysis of the Medici family has influenced contemporary financial analytics[17], which processes and analyzes billions of transactions to inform judgments about the world economy.

However, modern data analytics started to take shape only in the mid-20th century, with the appearance of computers. In the 1960s, the invention of structured data and canned reports (which are pre-designed and pre-formatted reports that are often included

16. Plester, V., Huylebrouck, H. 1999. The Ishango Artefact: The Missing Base12 Link. Forma, 14, 1999, pp. 339–346.

17. Genc, S.Y. 2021. *The Medici's Influence: Revival of Political and Financial Thought in Europe.* Belleten, April 2021, DOI: 10.37879/belleten.2021.29.

in software applications) represented a significant step in the evolution of data analytics, as this made the processing of large datasets feasible. Fast forward to the 1980s and we witness the emergence of relational databases, which are databases structured to recognize relations between stored items of information. Relational databases have symbols being organized into a collection of relations, often expressed in tabular form.[18] They allow users to retrieve data using Structured Query Language (SQL). This was a revolutionary moment, as it democratized data access, making data analysis more accessible and widespread.

The late 1980s and early 1990s saw another key development with the proposal of the "data warehouse" concept. Proposed by William H. Inmon, data warehouses are systems optimized for reporting and data analysis, allowing for a significant increase in the amount of data collected. The 1990s also introduced us to data mining - the process of discovering patterns in large datasets. This development allowed for a different way to analyze data, providing the opportunity for unexpected yet beneficial results. Today data mining is used in a variety of sectors, including retail, financial services, insurance, manufacturing, entertainment, and healthcare. Finding connections and patterns that would otherwise be challenging can be accomplished with the help of data mining. Many organizations utilize this technology because it helps them understand their clients better and make more informed marketing decisions.[19]

But the biggest change was yet to come – the internet. Larry Page and Sergey Brin developed the Google search engine, capable

---

18. Darwen, H. 2010. An Introduction to Relational Database Theory. Hugh Darwen & Ventus Publishing ApS, ISBN 978-87-7681-500-4.

19. Ramageri, B.M. 2010. *Data Mining Techniques and Applications*. Indian Journal of Computer Science and Engineering, Vol. 1, No.4, 301-305.

of processing and analyzing big data on distributed computers. With the onset of the internet, data analytics truly took off! The early 2010s witnessed the rise of cloud-based data warehouses like Amazon Redshift and Google BigQuery, democratizing access to big data analysis. [20]

At the same time, an interesting phenomenon appeared called data deluge, driven by several factors depicted in Figure 1.1. A data deluge is a situation when a huge amount of data is created, much more than it can be managed and processed. For example, in today's world, a lot of data is generated from social media, smart grids, video rendering, and other sources as illustrated in Figure 1.1.

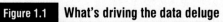

Figure 1.1   What's driving the data deluge

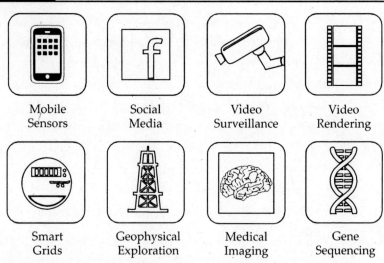

| Mobile Sensors | Social Media | Video Surveillance | Video Rendering |
| Smart Grids | Geophysical Exploration | Medical Imaging | Gene Sequencing |

Source: Long, C. et al. 2015. Data Science & Big Data Analytics: Discovering, Analyzing, Visualizing and Presenting Data. John Wiley & Sons, Inc., Canada. ISBN: 978-1-118-87613-8.

20. Lefebvre, H., Legner, C., Fadler, M. 2021. *Data democratization: toward a deeper understanding.* Proceedings of The Forty-Second International Conference on Information Systems, Austin 2021.

Many of the items in Figure 1.1 are driving the acceleration of data creation. Among the big data sources with the quickest rate of growth are social media and genetic sequencing, which are instances of non-traditional data sources being analyzed. For example, advertisements for bridal gowns, wedding preparation, or name-changing services would appear in response to an update indicating that a lady had changed her relationship status from "single" to "engaged."[21]

Today, data analytics has become an integral part of our lives, both in business and personal spheres. The industry has exploded, with the market for big data and business analytics expected to hit $420.98 billion by 2027[22]. In a world where data analytics is present in every aspect of life, from business intelligence to personalized services, we are constantly tapping into the power of data to make informed decisions.[23] Further advancements in AI and machine learning will take place in the future, promising an even more exciting chapter in the history of data analytics. The journey, it seems, is just getting started!

21. Long, C. et al. 2015. *Data Science & Big Data Analytics: Discovering, Analyzing, Visualizing and Presenting Data.* John Wiley & Sons, Inc., Canada. ISBN: 978-1-118-87613-8.

22. Pramod, B., Shadaab, K., Vineet, K. 2021. *Big Data and Business Analytics Market Report. Global Opportunity Analysis and Industry Forecast, 2021–2030.* Allied Market Research, Report Code: A05903. URL: https://www.alliedmarketresearch.com/big-data-and-business-analytics-market .

23. Nanda, P., Kumar, V. 2022. *Information Processing and Data Analytics for Decision Making: A Journey From Traditional to Modern Approaches.* Information Resources Management Journal, Volume 35, Issue 2. DOI: 10.4018/IRMJ.291693.

1.5 Key Concepts in Data Analytics

Now let's dive into some of the key concepts of data analytics.

There are four main types of analytics: **descriptive, diagnostic, predictive, and prescriptive.** [24] Each one of these plays a unique role in how we understand and utilize data.

Firstly, **descriptive analytics** tell us "what happened". This type of analytics involves analyzing historical data to understand changes over time. Whether it's website traffic, sales trends, or social media engagement, descriptive analytics are your go-to for understanding past behavior.

Secondly, we have **diagnostic analytics**, which aims to answer the question "Why did it happen?". Here, the goal is to dig deeper into data to understand the root cause of a particular outcome. It's like being a data detective, looking for clues and connections in a sea of information.

Third on our list is **predictive analytics.** You guessed it! This type involves making educated guesses about the future. It answers the question "What could happen?". By analyzing trends and patterns from the past, predictive analytics can forecast future trends, allowing businesses to make proactive decisions.

Lastly, we have **prescriptive analytics,** which tells us "What should we do about it?". This type uses optimization and simulation algorithms to advise on possible outcomes. Think of it like a sophisticated data crystal ball, providing guidance on how to best respond to predicted future scenarios.

24. Moreira, João Mendes, André C. P. L. F. de Carvalho, and Tomáš Horváth. 2019. *A General Introduction to Data Analytics.* John Wiley & Sons, Inc.

Another key concept in data analytics is understanding the strategic impact of data on organizational goals.[25] That means identifying how data can be utilized to drive business objectives and planning accordingly. This process involves building a data analytics strategic roadmap, which outlines action steps to realize business goals using data and analytics objectives.

Now, let's take a moment to talk about big data. **Big data** are those data sets whose dispersion, size, diversity, and/or timeliness necessitate the use of novel technical architectures and analytics in order to provide insights that open up new avenues for generating benefits for the company.[26] It's all about managing data that exceeds the storage or processing capacity of traditional systems. With the advent of the internet and the digital age, big data has become increasingly relevant and impactful.

Big data can take many different forms, including text files, multimedia files, genetic maps, financial data, and others. The majority of big data is unstructured or semi-structured, in contrast to much of the traditional data analysis carried out by enterprises, necessitating the use of new processing and analysis methods and tools. Four different types of data structures are depicted in Figure 1.2. Non-structured data categories will account for 80–90% of future data expansion[27] .

25. Demir, A. 2017. *Importance of Data Analysis on Achieving the Organizational Goals during The Short Term Strategic Plan: Case of Service Quality and Students' Satisfaction Level at Ishik University.* International Journal of Social Sciences & Educational Studies.ISSN 2520-0968 (Online), ISSN 2409-1294 (Print), March 2017, Vol.3, No.3.

26. Manyika, J., Chui, M., Brown, B., Bughin, J., Dobbs, R., Roxburgh, C., Byer, A.H.. 2011. *Big data: The next frontier for innovation, competition, and productivity.* McKinsey&Company.

27. Gantz, D.R.J. 2013. *The Digital Universe in 2020: Big Data, Bigger Digital Shadows, and Biggest Growth in the Far East.* IDC, 2013.

Figure 1.2   **Different types of data structures**

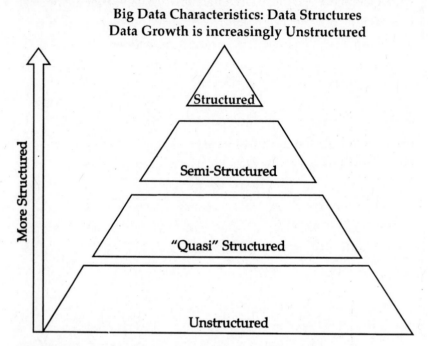

Source: Long, C. et al. 2015. Data Science & Big Data Analytics: Discovering, Analyzing, Visualizing and Presenting Data. John Wiley & Sons, Inc., Canada. ISBN: 978-1-118-87613-8.

The four are distinct, but they are frequently combined. Call logs for a software support call center, for instance, might be kept in a traditional Relational Database Management System (RDBMS). Time stamps, machine type, problem type, and operating system are examples of common structured data that the RDBMS may hold in relation to the support calls. Furthermore, it is probable that the system will contain unstructured, quasi-structured, or semi-structured data, such as free-call log information extracted from an email ticket describing the issue, customer chat history, or an audio file or transcript of a phone call detailing the technical issue and how it was resolved. The call center data's unstructured, quasi-, and semi-structured data offer an abundance of insights. [28]

Lastly, it is important to mention the concept of **data literacy** or, as some might call it, learning to "speak data."[29] This refers to the ability to read, understand, and communicate with data. It's about being fluent in the language of data, and capable of interpreting and applying data for value in context.

So, that's a whirlwind tour of some key concepts in data analytics. Remember, data analytics isn't just about numbers and algorithms, it's about finding stories in the data, making informed decisions, and unlocking potential. The world of data is rich and diverse, just waiting for you to dive in and explore!

28. Long, C. et al. 2015. *Data Science & Big Data Analytics: Discovering, Analyzing, Visualizing and Presenting Data.* John Wiley & Sons, Inc., Canada. ISBN: 978-1-118-87613-8.

29. Koltay, T. 2019. *Data literacy in academia: Basics and pedagogical views.* Opus et Educatio 6(4), DOI:10.3311/ope.343.

Quiz

---

1. **What is data analytics primarily about?**

   a. Uploading pictures and music

   b. Making sense of raw information

   c. Sifting for gold

   d. Collecting data

2. **What is the main difference between data analysis and data analytics?**

   a. Data analysis is about finding patterns in data, while data analytics is about applying those patterns to inform business decisions.

   b. Data analysis is about collecting and cleaning data, while data analytics is about analyzing and interpreting data.

   c. Data analysis is a one-time task, while data analytics is an ongoing process.

   d. Data analysis is used by businesses, while data analytics is used by individuals.

3. **Which of these is NOT a step in the typical data analytics process?**

    a. Looking for the necessary data

    b. Redoing the preprocessing tasks

    c. Posting data on social media

    d. Tuning the hyper-parameters of each method

4. **How is the process of data analytics best described?**

    a. A one-time task

    b. A linear process

    c. A cyclical, iterative process

    d. A random process

5. **How do data analysts utilize tools like R, Python, and Tableau?**

    a. They avoid using them in favor of manual calculations.

    b. They use them to decrease the data size.

    c. They leverage them to dive deep into data and extract insights.

    d. They consider them redundant in modern data analysis.

6. **How do the roles of a data scientist and data analyst typically differ?**

    a. They are identical roles.

    b. A data scientist's role is typically broader.

    c. A data analyst's role is typically broader.

    d. A data analyst often begins their career as a data scientist.

7. **What type of questions does data science typically answer, compared to data analytics?**

    a. Broader, more open-ended questions

    b. Specific, defined questions

    c. Both answer the same type of questions

    d. Neither field answers questions

8. **Which of the following best describes the key skills and tools that differ between data analytics and data science?**

    a. Both require the same set of skills and tools

    b. Only data analytics requires programming skills

    c. Data science often utilizes machine learning and data mining, while data analytics usually does not.

    d. Data analytics often utilizes machine learning and data mining, while data science usually does not.

9. **According to the text, what role does data analytics play in businesses?**

   a. It has no significant role.

   b. It acts like the compass, guiding businesses with evidence-based strategies.

   c. It is only used for processing customer feedback.

   d. It's primarily used for data protection.

10. **How does data analytics help businesses in terms of consumer feedback?**

   a. It converts consumer feedback into profitable insights.

   b. It allows businesses to ignore consumer feedback.

   c. It has no impact on consumer feedback.

   d. It turns consumer feedback into a source of data protection.

Answers	1 – b	2 – a	3 – c	4 – c	5 – c
	6 – b	7 – a	8 – c	9 – b	10 – a

Chapter Summary

◆ Data analytics involves the collection, pre-processing, transformation, modeling, and interpretation of data to draw conclusions, predict future trends, and guide decision-making. Particularly in the current digital era, data analytics provides important insights that are essential for business growth.

◆ The process of data analytics comprises five stages: identifying, collecting, cleaning, analyzing, and interpreting data. It's a cyclical and evolving process, using various tools like spreadsheets, R, Python, RapidMiner, Hadoop, Spark, Tableau, and KNIME.

◆ Data analytics and data science, while both dealing with data, have distinct focuses and applications. Data analytics is about analyzing data to answer specific questions and the role of data science is broader, often utilizing machine learning algorithms and data mining activities.

◆ Data analytics helps drive business growth by providing valuable insights, the importance of data analytics in this digital era being poised to grow further.

◆ The story of modern data analytics started to form in the mid-20th century with the advent of computers, structured data, canned reports, and relational databases that democratized data access.

◆ The internet era brought revolutionary change, with Google's search engine capable of processing and analyzing big data in distributed computers. The early 2010s saw the rise of cloud-based data warehouses, further democratizing access to big data analysis.

◆ While data science and data analytics both work with data, data science plays a larger role, while data analytics concentrates on providing answers to particular problems.

◆ Data analytics is based on four main types of analytics: prescriptive (what should be done about it), predictive (what might happen), diagnostic (the reason for its happening), and descriptive (what has happened).

◆ Some key concepts of data analytics include the four types of data analytics, respectively descriptive, diagnostic, predictive, and prescriptive, the term 'big data' and 'data literacy'.

This page is intentionally left blank

Chapter **2**

Data Collection and Management

Data analytics, the science of interpreting raw data to extract meaningful insights, is crucial in our increasingly data-centric world. At its heart lies the process of data collection and management, the focus of this pivotal chapter. A journey of discovery, beginning with the diverse sources of data and the various types of data, lays the groundwork for understanding the complex tapestry of information we work with. Building on this, we delve into the crucial process of data preprocessing, which ensures data integrity and usability. Finally, we explore the principles and technologies underpinning data storage and retrieval, equipping you to effectively manage and utilize the data in your analytic pursuits.

The key learning objectives of this chapter should include the reader's understanding of the following:

- Planning for data collection

- Classification of sources of data into internal and external at a company level

- Common categories of sources of data

- Various types of data: quantitative and qualitative, primary and secondary, structured and unstructured

- Data preprocessing and its importance in data analytics

- Data storage and retrieval and its importance in data analytics

2.1 Planning for Data Collection

Planning for data collection involves taking into account the following fundamental factors to guarantee the validity and reliability of the data to be gathered and analyzed: the purpose of the data collection, the methodology, the resources, and the timing of the data collection.[30] Figure 2.1 depicts the four key considerations for data collection.

30. Barrech, K. et al. 2020. IOM Monitoring and Evaluation Guidelines. International Organization for Migration (IOM), Geneva. ISBN 978-92-9268-016-9

Figure 2.1	Key considerations when planning for data collection

Source: Barrech, K. et al. 2020. IOM Monitoring and Evaluation Guidelines. International Organization for Migration (IOM), Geneva. ISBN 978-92-9268-016-9.

Regarding investigating the purpose for data collection, the following questions should be asked[31]:

- Is the data being collected for evaluation or monitoring purposes?

- What information is most important?

- What are the goals, results, products, and tasks that are being watched over or assessed?

- What long-term and intermediate-term outcomes are anticipated?

---

31. Barrech, K. et al. 2020. IOM Monitoring and Evaluation Guidelines. International Organization for Migration (IOM), Geneva. ISBN 978-92-9268-016-9.

- Which informational requirements from the stakeholders will the data meet?

When considering methodologies and methods for data collection, it's crucial to address several aspects such as:

- Identifying the data source

- Determining the frequency of data collection

- Understanding how the data will be measured

- Deciding who will collect the data

- Choosing the right methodology to design the appropriate data collection tools

Furthermore, it is also essential to:

- Define the criteria and questions addressed by the data collection tools

- Identify the type of data necessary to meet the information needs

- Determine if multiple data sources are required

- Recognize existing data types

Resources are crucial for the execution of data collection. One of the key considerations is to assess if sufficient staff and budget are available for data collection[32]. Finally, the usefulness of the data and the resources' availability may be impacted by timing. It is important to prevent the outdating of data.

---

32. Barrech, K. et al. 2020. IOM Monitoring and Evaluation Guidelines. International Organization for Migration (IOM), Geneva. ISBN 978-92-9268-016-9.

2.2 Sources of Data

Data has become an essential component in the digital age, intimately intertwined into the fabric of our lives and of enterprises. A dense informational network is created with each interaction, click, and passing second. This large collection of data, which consists of structured, semi-structured, and unstructured information, acts as a crucial reservoir, triggering important insights and decisions in a variety of businesses.[33]

It's not simple to categorize these enormous data sources, but let's break it down. Data is categorized as either internal or external in the business world. Internal data, which contains crucial information on operations, transactions, and other departmental insights like sales, finance, and HR, is the lifeblood of your business. On the other hand, external data is like the oxygen that keeps your business alive; it is derived from a variety of sources like censuses, social media, and economic indicators.

There are a wide variety of data sources available. We may divide them into several separate groups, each of which exhibits particular characteristics and calls for a particular set of analytical techniques. These key categories include, among others:

Business data: This comprises extensive information about your clients, sales, inventories, and other things. Usually, relational databases or data warehouses hold these details. Such data promote effective analysis because they are well-organized[34].

33. Sarker, I.H. 2021. Data Science and Analytics: An Overview from Data-Driven Smart Computing, Decision-Making and Applications Perspective. SN COMPUT. SCI. 2, 377 (2021). https://doi.org/10.1007/s42979-021-00765-8 .

34. Sarker, I.H. 2021. Data Science and Analytics: An Overview from Data-Driven Smart Computing, Decision-Making and Applications Perspective. SN COMPUT. SCI. 2, 377

Web and social media data: This is the data from websites, social media platforms, and online forums. In the modern, digitally interconnected world, interactions across these platforms considerably add to the overall data pool. Processing and analyzing this data, which is frequently semi-structured or unstructured, calls for sophisticated tools and methods.

Sensor data: As a result of the Internet of Things (IoT) revolution, sensors are generating data in real-time at an astounding rate. Industries including healthcare, manufacturing, and transportation eagerly assimilate this data.[35] A high-level view of a typical IoT architecture that shows the data flow is given in Fig. 2.2.

Figure 2.2   Internet of Things (IoT) architecture

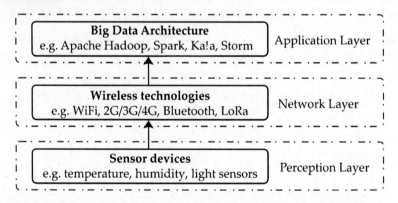

Source: Teh, H.Y., Kempa-Liehr, A.W., Wang, K.I.-K. 2020. Sensor data quality: a systematic review. Journal of Big Data, (2020) 7:11. DOI: https://doi.org/10.1186/s40537-020-0285-1.

(2021). https://doi.org/10.1007/s42979-021-00765-8 .

35. Sayantan Khanra, Amandeep Dhir, A. K. M. Najmul Islam & Matti Mäntymäki. 2020. Big data analytics in healthcare: a systematic literature review. Enterprise Information Systems, 14:7, 878-912, DOI: 10.1080/17517575.2020.1812005.

A physical sensor measures and gathers data at the Perception layer, such as a temperature or humidity sensor. After that, the readings are sent via the network layer, which uses wireless technologies like WiFi, 2G, 3G, 4G, Bluetooth, and LoRa to decide which routes to transport the sensor data[36]. After data is received from the network layer, it is processed, stored, and subjected to predictive analytics3[37]in the Application layer. Spark, Kafka, Apache Hadoop, and other big data architectures are used in the design and implementation of the application layer.

Publicly available data: Such data are routinely made available by governments, academic institutions, and other entities. This wide variety of data, which includes everything from census information to weather reports, is a valuable resource for scholars and data analysts.[38]

Big data: This term refers to data sets that are so large or intricate that conventional data processing techniques fail. Such datasets can include both structured and unstructured data and are quickly generated from a variety of sources, including social media feeds, weblogs, or artificial data.[39]

---

36. Teh, H.Y., Kempa-Liehr, A.W., Wang, K.I.-K. 2020. Sensor data quality: a systematic review. Journal of Big Data, (2020) 7:11. DOI: https://doi.org/10.1186/s40537-020-0285-1.

37. Christ, M., Krumeich, J., Kempa-Liehr, A.W. 2016. Integrating predictive analytics into complex event processing by using conditional density estimations. In: IEEE 20th international enterprise distributed object computing workshop (EDOCW). In: IEEE computer society, Los Alamitos, CA, USA; 2016. pp. 1–8. https://doi.org/10.1109/EDOCW.2016.7584363.

38. Institute of Medicine and National Research Council. 2002. Integrity in Scientific Research: Creating an Environment That Promotes Responsible Conduct. Washington, DC: The National Academies Press. https://doi.org/10.17226/10430.

39. Sivarajah, U., Kamal, M.M., Irani, Z. and Weerakkody, V. 2017. Critical analysis of Big Data challenges and analytical methods. Journal of Business Research, Volume 70, January 2017, Pages 263-286.

Fun Fact

Did you know that there is an amazing amount of data created on the internet every minute? For example, in 2021, people tweeted 575,000 times and posted 167 million videos on TikTok![40]

As a whole, the field of data sources for analytics is both diverse and fascinating. When analysts and data scientists use these numerous sources, the result is a plethora of deeper insights that drive innovation and decision-making in a variety of industries. These data sources have a lot of promise for major insights and information, despite the storage and processing difficulties they pose, which can lead to groundbreaking discoveries.

2.3 Types of Data

It is crucial that we become familiar with data classifications as we start our research of the large field of data analytics. In data analytics, there are primarily two categories of data: quantitative and qualitative.

Quantitative data: Numerical data that can be quickly measured, analyzed, and visually displayed is referred to as quantitative data. Examples of this structured data type include the number of visitors to a website or the local temperature. These numbers can also be divided into discrete or continuous data. Continuous

40. Karinshak, E., Jin, Y. 2023. AI-driven disinformation: a framework for organizational preparation and response. Emerald Publishing Limited. Journal of communication management, 23 Oct 2023, Vol. 27, Issue 4, pages 539 - 562. ISSN: 1363254X. DOI: 10.1108/JCOM-09-2022-0113.

data, like temperature measurements, can take on any value within a certain range. Contrarily, discrete data consists of certain numerical values, such as the number of people in a certain space.

Qualitative data: Contrary to its quantitative counterpart, qualitative data is either unstructured or semi-structured. Text, photos, audio, and video all fall under this type of data. Examples of this kind of content include customer reviews on e-commerce websites or pictures uploaded to social networking sites. Although measuring and analyzing qualitative data has historically been difficult, advances in big data technologies and machine learning methods have significantly increased our capacity to extract valuable insights from such data.[41]

Quick Tips

When exploring data analytics, keep in mind that the tools and methods you use should be appropriate for the type of data you are working with. A deliberate combination will improve the precision and applicability of your insights while also streamlining the analytical process.

Data can also be categorized as primary or secondary. **Primary data** is unprocessed information that is received straight from the source, such as survey results from customers. In contrast, **secondary data** is information that has been processed and is typically derived from primary data, such as produced reports.

The data landscape has undergone tremendous change as a result of big data. Large datasets that can't be effectively processed

---

41. Sivarajah, U., Kamal, M.M., Irani, Z. and Weerakkody, V. 2017. Critical analysis of Big Data challenges and analytical methods. Journal of Business Research, Volume 70, January 2017, Pages 263-286.

by traditional data processing techniques are referred to as "big data." Social media sites, Internet of Things (IoT) devices, and machine logs are just a few examples of the sources from which this data may come. Big data analysis offers priceless insights that can improve decision-making procedures[42].

Data can also take the form of **cross-sectional data**, which is collected at a certain time, **time-series data**, where each data point is associated with a particular timestamp, or **pooled data**, which combines cross-sectional and time-series data.

Finally, **structured** and **unstructured** forms of data can be distinguished. Unstructured data includes material like social media posts or articles and is less ordered than structured data, which is found in traditional databases.

Understanding the various data types represents an initial but crucial phase in the data analytics process. The ultimate goal of such an attempt is to make it possible to provide precise predictions, make educated decisions, and finally provide a significant benefit to enterprises or research operations. The steps taken to achieve this objective can be seen as a journey that gradually reveals the data analytics' complexity and simplifies the ideas into understandable parts.

2.4 Data Preprocessing

The old phrase "data is the new gold" is becoming more and more true as the digital era develops. Raw data does not, however,

---

42. Cote, C. 2021. 4 Types of Data Analytics to Improve Decision-Making. Harvard Business School Online. URL: https://online.hbs.edu/blog/post/types-of-data-analysis .

immediately offer the value it may possess, just like unprocessed gold. A key step in realizing this potential is data preprocessing, which is a group of techniques, like missing value imputation and outlier elimination, for improving the raw data quality.[43]

For data preprocessing, the data must be compatible with the requirements of the intended data analysis procedures. This process is known as data transformation. In addition to dealing with dataset transformation and data preparation, data preprocessing also aims to increase the effectiveness of knowledge discovery[44].

Data preprocessing consists of four main tasks: – the task of **data cleaning, integration, transformation,** and **reduction**.

Data cleaning entails locating and fixing errors within a dataset to guarantee that the information used in the analysis is free of noise (i.e. meaningless data or that data which the analyst chooses not to fit, with the assumption that there is a model that explains the rest of the data[45]), free of outliers (questionable observations or measurements because they deviate significantly from the vast majority of the observations in size or number[46]),

43. Fan, C., Wang, J., Chen, M., Wang, X. 2021. A Review on Data Preprocessing Techniques Toward Efficient and Reliable Knowledge Discovery From Building Operational Data. Frontiers in Energy Research, Volume 9, DOI:10.3389/fenrg.2021.652801.

44. Alasadi, S.A., Bhaya, W.S. 2017. Review of Data Preprocessing Techniques in Data Mining. Journal of Engineering and Applied Sciences 12(16): 4102-4107. ISBN: 1816-949X.

45. Scales, J.A. 1998. What is noise? Geophysics, Vol. 63, No.4 (July-August 1998), p. 1122-1124.

46. Cousineau, D., Chartier, S. 2010. Outliers detection and treatment: a review. International Journal of Psychological Research, 3 (1), 59-68.

free of incomplete records, and inconsistent data.[47] To find these errors, many methods including data validation, data screening, and data diagnosis are used. De-duplication is also an important stage because it gets rid of redundant data. Depending on the situation and the required standards of data quality, the management of missing data and outliers is also handled, either by imputation or exclusion.

Especially for big data, several cleansing methods have been designed over the years. Some of the most famous ones are given in Table 2.1.

Table 2.1   Data cleansing methods for big data

Methods	Key Features	Execution Method	Approach
Cleanix	Scalability, unification, and usability	Parallel	Rule selection
SCARE	Scalability	Parallel	Machine learning technique
KATARA	Easy specification, pattern validation, data annotation	Sequential	Knowledge-base and crowdsourcing
BigDansing	Efficiency, scalability, and ease of use	Parallel	Rule specification

Source: Ridzuan, F., Zainon, W.M.N.W. 2019. A Review on Data Cleansing Methods for Big Data. Procedia Computer Science 161 (2019) 731-738. 10.1016/j. procs.2019.11.177.

---

47. Alasadi, S.A., Bhaya, W.S. 2017. Review of Data Preprocessing Techniques in Data Mining. Journal of Engineering and Applied Sciences 12(16): 4102-4107. ISBN: 1816-949X.

Well-organized datasets have a distinct structure and are simple to work with, analyze, and visualize.[48] Next, we have **data integration**, which is the process of merging data from various sources into a single view. This is done to guarantee effective data management, produce insightful discoveries, and produce actionable intelligence. Data ingestion is the first step in the data integration process, which also involves steps like cleansing, ETL (Extract, Transform, Load) mapping, and transformation. This procedure ultimately enables analytical tools to produce effective business intelligence.

For example, in the field of biological research, data integration involves sharing data, integrating it, and labeling it to ensure repeatability of analysis and interpretation of experimental results.[49] This process is crucial in genomics since it calls for the integration of massive datasets from multiple domains.

Data transformation, a critical component of preprocessing, may comprise actions like standardizing data scales, encoding categorical data, and creating new predictive features from the already existing ones through feature engineering[50]. Data transformation is vital in a data-driven company, aiding in increasing revenue, improving customer service, enhancing operating efficiencies, and boosting profitability[51].

48. Wickham, H. 2014. Tidy data. Journal of Statistical Software 14(10), DOI:10.18637/jss.v059.i10 .

49. Lapatas, V., Stefanidakis, M., Jimenez, R.C. et al. 2015. Data integration in biological research: an overview. Journal of Biological Result-Thessaloniki 22, 9 (2015). DOI: https://doi.org/10.1186/s40709-015-0032-5.

50. Liu, H. 2018. Feature Engineering for Machine Learning and Data Analytics. Chapman & Hall/ CRC Press. ISBN 9780367571856.

51. Brown, S. 2020. How to build a data-driven company. MIT Management Sloan School. URL: https://mitsloan.mit.edu/ideas-made-to-matter/how-to-build-a-data-driven-company .

In data analytics, the term **data reduction** refers to the act of simplifying, reducing, or otherwise transforming huge, complex datasets into a more manageable and comprehendible form with minimal information loss. It is a crucial phase in the processing and analysis of data since it reduces storage needs, increases efficiency, and gets rid of redundant information[52]. It helps data analysts and scientists make sense of the data and extract valuable insights efficiently.

Overall, data preprocessing supports the dependability and robustness of the results of the subsequent data analytics, just like a solid foundation supports the stability of a home, and it is a fundamental phase in data analysis that enables the efficient and useful use of data. It plays a crucial part in data-driven decision-making by assisting in the optimization of the data's structure and quality, ensuring that it is prepared for additional analytical procedures.

2.5 Data Storage and Retrieval

The amount of data collected and used on a daily basis in our increasingly digital world is growing at an unheard-of rate, from the moment we get up to the moment we go to bed. The data generated, whether it is from using digital assistants like Alexa or engaging with material on different social media platforms, is

52. Biswas, A., Dutta, S., Turton, T.L., Ahrens, J. 2022. Sampling for Scientific Data Analysis and Reduction. In: Childs, H., Bennett, J.C., Garth, C. (eds) In Situ Visualization for Computational Science. Mathematics and Visualization. Springer, Cham. DOI: https://doi.org/10.1007/978-3-030-81627-8_2 .

managed, stored, and retrieved as necessary rather than existing aimlessly. This process is the foundation of data analytics.[53]

We can compare data storage and retrieval to a vast digital library to better grasp the complexities involved. But instead of actual books, this library is made up of bits and bytes that are orderly placed on digital shelves and are available whenever needed. The methods used to store these "digital books" are primarily determined by the type of information being gathered[54].

For instance, administrative functions frequently use manual methods to collect data, whereas modern facilities typically rely on automated or semi-automated technologies. Similar comparisons might be made between this and a humanly operated book recording system in an antiquated library and an automated system in a modern library.

The core idea of the digital library is the same whether it's a physical book or an electronic book: the material must be kept in a systematic way to make retrieval easy. Storage systems must be able to manage a wide variety of data formats in the context of data analytics, from straightforward text files and intricately structured databases to a sizable amount of unstructured text data found on websites and social media platforms[55]. As a result, in order to accommodate the various "genres" of data we acquire, our data storage system needs to be both extensive and flexible.

---

53. Tsyen, N., Chan, T. 2016. Defining and Conceptualizing Actionable Insight: A Conceptual Framework for Decision-centric Analytics. Proceedings of The Australasian Conference on Information Systems, Adelaide, 2016.

54. National Cooperative Highway Research Program (NCHRP). 2003. Report 512: Accelerated Pavement Testing: Data Guidelines. National Academies of Sciences, Engineering, and Medicine. Washington, DC: The National Academies Press. https://doi.org/10.17226/21958.

55. ChengXiang Zhai,Sean Massung. 2016. Text Data Management and Analysis: A Practical Introduction to Information Retrieval and Text Mining. Association for Computing Machinery and Morgan & Claypool. DOI: https://doi.org/10.1145/2915031.

Our capacity for data storage should grow along with the flood of data. Data storage technologies, such as networked computer systems, disk storage, data storage, and retrieval software[56], must be continually invested in as a result. Data retrieval is a strategic game of hide-and-seek run by storage engines. These engines may be tailored for transactional workloads or analytics, but what sets them apart is their speedy access to and retrieval of stored data.

 Consider as an example a company that analyzes social media data to detect new fashion trends. Utilizing sophisticated algorithms, it combs through a vast number of posts daily. Their data is organized in a layered storage system, categorized by fashion types and further divided by apparel, accessories, colors, and public sentiment. When a trend, such as "chunky sneakers", surges in mentions, their retrieval system efficiently locates all related mentions across various social media platforms, distinguishing between different types of references, from tweets to detailed blog reviews or Instagram images.

Although the procedures for storing and retrieving data may appear complicated, they are essential to data analytics. Effective data storage and retrieval systems help businesses and organizations harness the power of data to extract insights and make educated decisions[57], just like a well-organized library facilitates the spread of knowledge. It's important to understand the complicated trip each bit and byte takes from generation to storage and then retrieval as we go deeper into the world of data analytics.

56. LeSueur, J. 2012. Data Acquisition, Storage, and Retrieval (Chapter 12). Marketing Automation: Practical Steps to More Effective Direct Marketing. Wiley Online Library. https://doi.org/10.1002/9781119197782.ch12

57. ChengXiang Zhai, Sean Massung. 2016. Text Data Management and Analysis: A Practical Introduction to Information Retrieval and Text Mining. Association for Computing Machinery and Morgan & Claypool. DOI: https://doi.org/10.1145/2915031.

Quiz

1. **What is the analogy used to describe internal data in a corporate sphere?**

   a. The brain of the company

   b. The lungs of the company

   c. The lifeblood of the company

   d. The skeleton of the company

2. **What are the characteristics of business data?**

   a. Highly unorganized, making analysis complex

   b. Very organized, making analysis difficult

   c. Very organized, making analysis easy

   d. Moderately organized, making analysis moderate

3. **What is a defining feature of big data?**

   a. It refers to small, manageable datasets.

   b. It refers to data so vast that conventional data processing technologies can handle it easily.

   c. It refers to data so vast that conventional data processing technologies struggle with it.

   d. It refers only to structured data.

4. **Which category of data includes numbers and quantities, and can be easily measured, analyzed, and visualized?**

   a. Primary data

   b. Secondary data

   c. Quantitative data

   d. Qualitative data

5. **What is a key characteristic of qualitative data?**

   a. It includes text, images, audio, and video.

   b. It can take any value within a given range.

   c. It can only take certain values.

   d. It includes numbers and quantities.

6. **What is the distinction between primary and secondary data?**

   a. Primary data is processed, while secondary data is raw.

   b. Primary data is collected directly from the source, while secondary data is processed data.

   c. Primary data includes numbers, while secondary data includes text.

   d. Primary data can be visualized, while secondary data can't be visualized.

7. **What type of data is defined as extremely large datasets that traditional data processing tools cannot handle?**

    a. Time-series data

    b. Big data

    c. Pooled data

    d. Cross-sectional data

8. **Which data type resides in traditional databases and is highly organized?**

    a. Primary data

    b. Secondary data

    c. Unstructured data

    d. Structured data

9. **What are some techniques involved in detecting errors during the data cleaning process?**

    a. Data integration and feature selection

    b. Data validation, data screening, and data diagnosing

    c. Data transformation and feature engineering

    d. Data analysis and data presentation

10. **What does de-duplication in data cleaning refer to?**

    a. Standardizing data scales

    b. Dealing with missing data and outliers

    c. Removing unnecessary duplicate data

    d. Encoding categorical data

Answers	1 – c	2 – c	3 – c	4 – c	5 – a
	6 – b	7 – b	8 – d	9 – b	10 – c

Chapter Summary

◆ Several key considerations must be taken into account regarding planning for data collection such as purpose for data collection, methodology and methods for data collection, resources for data collection, and timing for data collection.

◆ Data sources can be classified into many categories, for example, internal and external, where internal data pertains to company operations and transactions, and external data comes from diverse sources like censuses, social media, and economic indicators.

◆ There are some other categories of data sources such as business data, web and social media data, sensor data, publicly available data, and big data.

◆ There are various types of data dealt with in analytics, including quantitative data, qualitative data, primary and secondary data, and structured and unstructured data.

◆ Big data can offer valuable insights for decision-making processes. Furthermore, the evolving capabilities in handling unstructured or semi-structured data like text, images, audio, and video have been pointed out, facilitated by advancements in machine learning and big data.

◆ Data preprocessing is the transformation of raw data into a suitable format for analysis. It includes data cleaning, data integration, data transformation, and data reduction.

◆ The process of data storage and retrieval is intricate: we can imagine an immense library where data 'books' are stored systematically to be easily retrieved when needed.

◆ The adaptability and robustness of data storage systems are important and they necessitate continual investment in technology, including networked computer systems, disk storage, and data storage/retrieval software, with a strong emphasis on security, archiving, and restoration systems.

Chapter **3**

Types of Data Analytics

D ata analytics, an essential tool in today's digital age, allows us to process vast amounts of information and extract insightful knowledge. In this chapter, we'll explore the four primary types of data analytics: descriptive, inferential, predictive, and prescriptive. Just like a skilled storyteller, each type paints a different part of the picture.

The key learning objective of this chapter is to understand more about the four types of data analytics

- Descriptive analytics which tells us what happened,

- Inferential analytics which offers insights on a larger population from a sample,

- Predictive analytics which forecasts what might happen in the future, and

- Prescriptive analytics which advises us on the course of action to take.

By understanding and applying these analytics types, we can navigate our complex business landscapes more effectively. We can utilize these to not only address our present scenarios but also anticipate the future and strategize accordingly [58]. So, brace yourselves as we step into the realm of the different types of data analytics, allowing it to illuminate our path and guide our decision-making.

3.1 Descriptive Analytics

"What happened?" is one of the fundamental questions we ask in our journey of understanding. This is where descriptive analytics, the foundation of all types of data analytics, comes into play.

The heartbeat of descriptive analytics is its ability to transform raw data into useful insights about past events. Whether it's a scientist piecing together research data or a business leader reviewing a quarter's sales, descriptive analytics offers a lens through which we can view and make sense of our world [59].

Consider a graph that shows the sales trend of a product over a year. What you are seeing is descriptive analytics in action! It uses statistical summaries to present an accurate picture of past

58. Tsyen, N., Chan, T. 2016. Defining and Conceptualizing Actionable Insight: A Conceptual Framework for Decision-centric Analytics. Proceedings of The Australasian Conference on Information Systems, Adelaide, 2016.

59. Ma, A. 2020. Making Data Reports Useful: From Descriptive to Predictive. National Library of Medicine. Cureus, v.12(10); 2020 October; e10920. URL: https://www.ncbi.nlm.nih.gov/pmc/articles/PMC7657442/

events and trends, setting the stage for other types of data analysis - predictive and prescriptive [60].

The real value of descriptive analytics, however, isn't just in looking back. Businesses, for instance, leverage it to inform strategies, drive decision-making, and ultimately improve performance [61]. It gives the context or the starting point from which other analytics techniques can build their predictions and prescriptions.

Unlike predictive analytics, descriptive analytics does not have a target variable. As a result, unsupervised learning is another name for descriptive analytics. Let's talk about the process. Descriptive analytics leverages different techniques and tools, including data categorization techniques such as hierarchical and non-hierarchical clustering algorithms and their variations, as well as association rule mining and sequence rule mining[62].

Data mining is a process that helps identify patterns and relationships in large datasets. The most important and well-known data mining technique is **association rule mining**. This technique's main goal is to uncover interesting relationships or shared patterns between sets of objects from relational or transactional databases.

---

60. Roy, D., Srivastava, R., Jat, M. & Karaca, M.S. 2022. A Complete Overview of Analytics Techniques: Descriptive, Predictive, and Prescriptive. Decision Intelligence Analytics and the Implementation of Strategic Business Management. EAI/Springer Innovations in Communication and Computing. Springer, Cham. https://doi.org/10.1007/978-3-030-82763-2_2 .

61. Cote, C. 2021. 4 Types of Data Analytics to Improve Decision-Making. Harvard Business School Online. URL: https://online.hbs.edu/blog/post/types-of-data-analysis

62. Sheik A. A., Selvakumar, S., Ramya, C. 2017. Descriptive Analytics. Volume: Applying Predictive Analytics Within the Service Sector. IGI Global book series Advances in Business Information Systems and Analytics (ABISA). ISSN: 2327-3275; eISSN: 2327-3283.

For example, if you have already bought a product, it is more likely that you will want to buy another product from the same category and not a product from a totally different category. Thus, purchasing a product from the same category with another product already purchased exemplifies an association rule.[63] Classification, telecommunications, clustering, market basket analysis, cross-marketing, loss-leader, catalog design, and other domains are among the many areas where association rule mining is frequently employed. The rules produced by association rule mining from the different application data can be used to learn new things. Some applications of association rule mining are medical treatments, weblog click streams, and customer shopping sequences.

There are two main techniques for mining association rules: the Apriori algorithm and the FP-Growth algorithm. From the massive transactional database, the apriori algorithm is used to extract frequently occurring item sets. It is the most effective algorithm for examining the objects' hidden relationships. An Apriori follows a bottom-up methodology[64].

The Frequent Pattern Growth algorithm is another name for the FP-Growth algorithm. It's an extra method of determining the most common item sets without having to create a candidate itemset. FP growth outpaces the Apriori method used for association rule mining. Every element in this algorithm is stored in a tree structure. The FP-Growth algorithm is used to mine

63. Ma, A. 2020. Making Data Reports Useful: From Descriptive to Predictive. National Library of Medicine. Cureus, v.12(10); 2020 October; e10920. URL: https://www.ncbi.nlm.nih.gov/pmc/articles/PMC7657442/

64. Sheik A. A., Selvakumar, S., Ramya, C. 2017. Descriptive Analytics. Volume: Applying Predictive Analytics Within the Service Sector. IGI Global book series Advances in Business Information Systems and Analytics (ABISA). ISSN: 2327-3275; eISSN: 2327-3283.

the association rules in two phases. Firstly, it creates an FP-tree, a dense data structure. Second, it takes the frequent itemsets straight out of the FP-tree.

The other main type of data mining is **sequence rules mining**. A subsequence of many database sequences is known as sequential rule mining. It is used to track things like what a customer has purchased from a store, how they have visited websites over time, phone call patterns, patient medical care, DNA sequences, and more.

Table 3.1 illustrates how data is represented in sequence rule mining. Suppose there are four sequences: S1, S2, S3, and S4, which are called the IDs in the table. The ID (S1, S2, S3, S4) is a pattern of the order in which the web pages are viewed. Some of the e-commerce URLs that customers view are a, b, c, d, e, f, g, and h. Suppose a stands for the homepage, b for electronics, c for a mobile page, d for a Samsung mobile, e stands for a mobile cover, f stands for the shopping basket, g for the order confirmation, and h for the option to continue shopping. Therefore S1 in the table shows one sequence of viewing the website wherein the customer first viewed the homepage and the mobile page, then Samsung mobile, followed by the order confirmation and continue shopping page (represented as {a, c}, {d}, {g}, {f} in the table.)

Table 3.1	Items with their sequences

ID	Sequences
S1	{a, c}, {d}, {g}, {f}
S2	{a, f}, {c}, {e,d, f, g}
S3	{e}, {a}, {g}, {c}
S4	{e, f, g}, {a}

Source: Sheik A. A., Selvakumar, S., Ramya, C. 2017. Descriptive Analytics. Volume: Applying Predictive Analytics Within the Service Sector. IGI Global book series Advances in Business Information Systems and Analytics (ABISA). ISSN: 2327-3275; eISSN: 2327-3283.

Some applications for sequence rule mining are quality assurance, prefetching web pages, analyzing customer behavior, embedded systems, and e-learning[65].

Clustering, on the other hand, groups similar data points, allowing us to understand customer behaviors or other phenomena in a segmented way [66]. The most significant challenge with unsupervised learning is clustering.[67] It does not employ the class label to identify the relevant structure among the dataset's components, the class labels being usually words that are given numerical values before being implemented in an algorithm. The goal of clustering is to put related objects together to form groups. The Manhattan, Euclidean, and Minkowski distances are the primary methods used to determine the items' similarities and differences.

65. Sheik A. A., Selvakumar, S., Ramya, C. 2017. Descriptive Analytics. Volume: Applying Predictive Analytics Within the Service Sector. IGI Global book series Advances in Business Information Systems and Analytics (ABISA). ISSN: 2327-3275; eISSN: 2327-3283.

66. Baesens, B. 2014. Analytics in a Big Data World: The Essential Guide to Data Science and its Applications. Willey, ISBN: 9781118892701.

67. Cote, C. 2021. 4 Types of Data Analytics to Improve Decision-Making. Harvard Business School Online. URL: https://online.hbs.edu/blog/post/types-of-data-analysis

The term "similarity" refers to the degree of similarity between things. The similarity measure is high when the distance is minimal. Conversely, when the distance is large, the similarity measure is little. The scale used to determine similarity is 0 to 1. The maximum degree of similarity exists within the cluster, while the maximum degree of dissimilarity exists between different clusters (lowest degree of similarity between the clusters).

Clustering can be hierarchical and non-hierarchical. Figure 3.1 illustrates the different types of clustering.

Figure 3.1   Different types of clustering

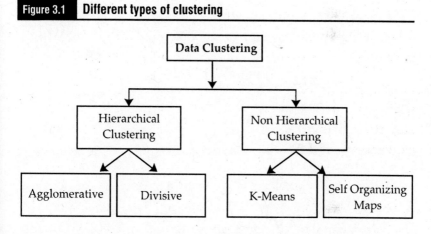

Source: Sheik A. A., Selvakumar, S., Ramya, C. 2017. Descriptive Analytics. Volume: Applying Predictive Analytics Within the Service Sector. IGI Global book series Advances in Business Information Systems and Analytics (ABISA). ISSN: 2327-3275; eISSN: 2327-3283.

Now, the beauty of descriptive analytics is its flexibility. It's like a Swiss army knife; you can use it in any industry. For instance, in healthcare, it can track disease trends, while in retail, it can highlight the most popular products. Every sector, every company, and even every individual can use descriptive analytics to gain insights into the past to prepare for the future.

Quick Tips

Keep it visual! Summarizing historical data is the core of descriptive analytics, and there's no better way to convey your results than with clear, concise visuals. Turn complicated data sets into stories that are easily understood at a glance by using graphs, charts, and dashboards. Pictures can tell you more about client behavior patterns and sales trends than thousands of spreadsheets can!

As we continue exploring descriptive analytics, remember this - it's not just about examining the past. It's about extracting insights that will help us navigate the present and predict the future. It's our first step in turning raw data into useful knowledge.

3.2 Inferential Analytics

Imagine you're a detective, but instead of solving crimes, you solve mysteries buried deep within chunks of data. This is the fascinating world of inferential analytics!

Inferential analytics, also known as inferential statistics, is a type of statistical analysis that uncovers hidden stories within data. It doesn't just describe the data in front of us, as in descriptive statistics; it goes beyond the present and makes educated predictions about larger data sets based on a smaller sample[68]. Picture this: you've gathered SAT scores from a few high school juniors in the U.S., and you're looking to infer the average

---

68. Pompeii, L.A. 1998. Inferential and advanced analysis of research data. AAOHN Journal., 1998 Oct;46(10):514-6.

SAT score of all 11th graders in the country. Or perhaps, you're investigating the relationship between SAT scores and family income. In both these scenarios, inferential analytics is your best tool!

Inferential statistics uses probability to form these educated predictions[69]. Think about weather forecasts, which predict future weather conditions based on present and past data. We don't have data for tomorrow's weather today, but we can infer it using sophisticated statistical methods.

One essential aspect of inferential analytics is the use of sample data, which represents a smaller section of the larger population. Why not study the entire population, you may wonder? It's simpler, less time-consuming, and more cost-effective! Sampling needs to be random and unbiased for the results to be valid[70]. As such, the careful selection of the sample and ensuring its representativeness of the larger population is vital.

Inferential analytics can be applied to the following types of data sets: cross-sectional time studies, retrospective data sets, and observational data sets [71].

69. Mukhopadhyay, N. 2000. Probability and Statistical Inference. Marcel Dekker, Inc., Volume 162. ISBN 0-8247-0379-0.

70. Williams, B.K., Brown, E.D. 2019. Sampling and analysis frameworks for inference in ecology. Wiley Online Library, Methods Ecol Evol. 2019;10:1832–1842. DOI: 10.1111/2041-210X.13279.

71. Bhattacherjee, A. 2012. Social science research: Principles, methods, and practices (2nd ed.). Textbooks Collection 3. Tampa Library at Digital Commons @ University of South Florida. https://digitalcommons.usf.edu/oa_textbooks/3.

In agriculture, inferential analytics has the potential to be revolutionary! Farmers can use sample data from a small crop area to estimate the overall health and prospective production of the farm. Precision agriculture is a method that makes farming more effective by using statistical models to forecast which regions would require more water, fertilizer, or insect control[72].

But like any exciting adventure, the journey through inferential analytics is also fraught with risks! Before delving into these risks, let's revise the concept of the hypothesis. A hypothesis is an educated guess about anything from your surroundings and it ought to be verifiable through observation or experimentation [73].

For example, there are two main types of inferential errors, corresponding to the situations in which we accept or not (on a correct ground or not) the alternative hypothesis which is a statement that contradicts or challenges the default assumption. Think of these errors as false alarms and missed opportunities, respectively. These types of errors are as follows: [74]

- Type I error, where we accept an alternative hypothesis when we shouldn't have, and

- Type II error, where we reject an alternative hypothesis when we should have accepted it.

72. Dekera, K., Eke, C.I. 2022. Smart farming prediction models for precision agriculture: a comprehensive survey. Springer, Artificial Intelligence Review. DOI: https://doi.org/10.1007/s10462-022-10266-6.

73. Singh, N. 2020. Hypothesis Testing in Data Science. The School of Computer Applications, Babu Banarasi Das University. DOI: 10.13140/RG.2.2.29097.62560.

74. Akobeng, A. 2016. Understanding type I and type II errors, statistical power and sample size. 2016 Foundation Acta Pædiatrica. Published by John Wiley & Sons Ltd. https://doi.org/10.1111/apa.13384

The most popular inferential statistical techniques are **regression, chi-square, t-test, analysis of variance (ANOVA), and time series**[75].

The **t-test**, often called the student's t-test, is a technique that's frequently used to evaluate a hypothesis in comparison to means or averages between the groups. [76]There are two types of T-tests: the directional or one-tailed test and the non-directional or two-tailed test. To comprehend the statistical differences between the means of the two groups, a non-directional or two-tailed test is utilized. The directional or one-tailed test, on the other hand, establishes if the mean of one group is statistically greater than the other. In summary, a t-test can be used to compare the means of two independent or dependent samples, to find the confidence interval for the sample mean, and to compare the sample mean value with the assumed mean. It should be mentioned that the purpose of this test is to test hypotheses.

Analysis of Variance (ANOVA): Multiple t-test results are equivalent to those of an ANOVA. As a result, this approach may be more effective and reduce the probability of erroneous results in addition to the decrease of the experiment-wise error. It can also handle problems with the validity of the intricate statistical result that is reached through the application of several t-tests.[77]

75. Taherdoost, H. 2020. Different Types of Data Analysis; Data Analysis Methods and Techniques in Research Projects. International Journal of Academic Research in Management (IJARM), Vol. 9, No. 1, 2020, Page: 1-9, ISSN: 2296-1747 © Helvetic Editions LTD, Switzerland.

76. Mukhopadhyay, N. 2000. Probability and Statistical Inference. Marcel Dekker, Inc., Volume 162. ISBN 0-8247-0379-0.

77. Akobeng, A. 2016. Understanding type I and type II errors, statistical power and sample size. 2016 Foundation Acta Pædiatrica. Published by John Wiley & Sons Ltd. https://doi.org/10.1111/apa.13384

Chi-square analysis is used to find correlations between two variables' categories. These two categorical variables come from the same population. Since this method is merely a test of proportions, it can only be used for nominal and ordinal data, unlike the other inferential tools that have been mentioned, which may be applied to interval and ratio data as well [78].

Regression analysis uses the values of one or more independent variables to forecast a dependent variable's value. As a result, this statistical method is similar to a correlation which shows the relationship between variables. Based on the main predictive object in regression, they differ, though. Estimating the likelihood and degree of anticipating the onset of particular criteria using a set of hypothesized risk factors is a significant use of regression analysis[79].

There are simple and multiple regressions. While multiple regressions may employ multiple independent variables to estimate and identify the dependent variable, the simple method just uses one[80].

Time series analysis can be used to examine variables that are constantly changing with respect to time. It works well with longitudinal research designs. In these systems, single units or objects are repeatedly calculated using vast numbers of observations at regular intervals. In many cases where the time

78. Taherdoost, H. 2020. Different Types of Data Analysis; Data Analysis Methods and Techniques in Research Projects. International Journal of Academic Research in Management (IJARM), Vol. 9, No. 1, 2020, Page: 1-9, ISSN: 2296-1747 © Helvetic Editions LTD, Switzerland.

79. Taherdoost, H. 2021. Handbook on Research Skills: The Essential Step-By-Step Guide on How to Do a Research Project. Amazon Kindle.

80. Marczyk, G. R., DeMatteo, D., Festinger, D. 2010. Essentials of research design and methodology (Vol. 2). John Wiley & Sons.

series compares many points in a single series, regression is utilized to examine the connection between time series[81].

As we've discovered, inferential analytics is a powerful tool that unlocks the secrets within data. It helps us make sense of the world around us, even when we only have a fraction of the data. Next time you see a weather forecast or read a study about population trends, remember the crucial role of inferential analytics!

3.3 Predictive Analytics

Imagine being able to foresee the future — not in a supernatural way but using the power of data. Welcome to the fascinating world of predictive analytics! This discipline, at the intersection of statistics, machine learning, and business intelligence, offers us a scientific glimpse into the future by analyzing current and historical data[82].

Predictive analytics is akin to a digital fortune-teller. It leverages a variety of techniques ranging from data mining to statistical modeling and machine learning to predict future outcomes based on historical and current data. It's akin to putting together a jigsaw puzzle where the pieces are the past and present data, and the completed image represents the future.

81. Bhattacherjee, A. 2012. Social science research: Principles, methods, and practices (2nd ed.). TextbooksCollection 3. Tampa Library at Digital Commons @ University of South Florida. https://digitalcommons.usf.edu/oa_textbooks/3.

82. Kumar, V. 2018. Predictive Analytics: A Review of Trends and Techniques. International Journal of Computer Applications 182(1):31-37, DOI: 10.5120/ijca2018917434.

From healthcare to finance, predictive analytics is transforming industries. In healthcare, predictive analytics can forecast patient health outcomes and improve service management. In business, it can anticipate customer behavior, optimize marketing strategies, and maximize profit. No matter the sector, predictive analytics provides the power to navigate future uncertainties with confidence and precision.

Fun Fact

Did you know that data analytics can forecast the popularity of songs? That's accurate! Through the analysis of beats, pace, lyrics, and even danceability, data analysts can predict which songs will top the charts with a remarkable degree of accuracy.

The process of predictive analytics begins with defining objectives and gathering data. This data is then cleaned, analyzed, and used to develop predictive models. These models can give a score indicating the likelihood of a certain event's occurrence. The higher the score, the greater the likelihood of that event occurring[83]. These models use historical and transactional data trends to uncover solutions to a wide range of scientific and business problems. These models are useful for determining the risks and opportunities that each client, employee, or manager of a company faces. Predictive analytics models have dominated as decision-support solutions have drawn more attention.

Let's imagine a retail company called XYZ. Predictive analytics can help analyze past sales, product preferences, and consumer behavior data to anticipate future buying patterns.

---

83. Kumar, V. 2018. Predictive Analytics: A Review of Trends and Techniques. International Journal of Computer Applications 182(1):31-37, DOI: 10.5120/ ijca2018917434.

This knowledge can guide strategies for product development, inventory management, and personalized marketing, making the business more proactive and efficient.[84]

The corporation uses the internet to manage its global retail business, selling a range of goods. Millions of customers look for products they want on the XYZ website. They search for the product's features, cost, and any available deals on the XYZ website. Many products have seasonal fluctuations in their sales. For instance, demand for geysers grows in the winter and air conditioners in the summer. Customers look for products based on the season. Here, the XYZ Company will gather all of the search information from clients regarding which products they are interested in purchasing throughout which seasons, the range of prices that a particular customer is willing to pay, how incentives on a product draw in customers, and what additional goods do consumers purchase in addition to a single item. Based on the gathered data, XYZ Company will utilize analytics to determine the needs of the client. It will determine which kind of advice will draw in each specific customer before contacting them via emails and messages. They will inform the client that the products they have on their website are eligible for this kind of offer.

The business will offer the other products that have been sold in combination to other consumers if the customer returns to the website to purchase that particular product. If a consumer begins making purchases regularly, the business may lower the offer or

84. Akobeng, A. 2016. Understanding type I and type II errors, statistical power and sample size. 2016 Foundation Acta Pædiatrica. Published by John Wiley & Sons Ltd. https://doi.org/10.1111/apa.13384

raise the price for that specific customer[85]. Predictive analytics has many more uses than this one; this is only an example.

Predictive analytics uses both historical and present data. The predictive analytics process is depicted in Figure 3.2, which is provided below.

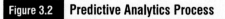

Figure 3.2   Predictive Analytics Process

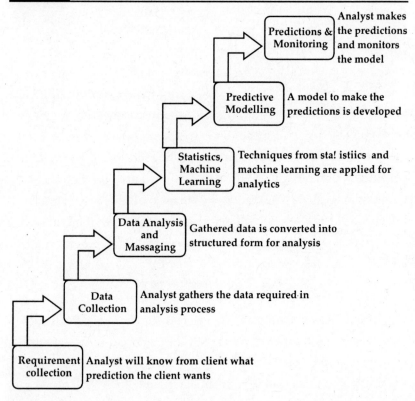

Source: Kumar, V. 2018. Predictive Analytics: A Review of Trends and Techniques. International Journal of Computer Applications 182(1):31-37, DOI: 10.5120/ijca2018917434.

85. Kumar, V. 2018. Predictive Analytics: A Review of Trends and Techniques. International Journal of Computer Applications 182(1):31-37, DOI: 10.5120/ijca2018917434.

It is necessary to establish the purpose of prediction before developing a predictive model. It is important to identify the kind of knowledge that will be acquired through the forecast. A pharmaceutical corporation, for instance, would like to know the anticipated sales of a drug in a specific area to prevent the drug's expiration. Once the analyst is aware of the needs of the client company, they will gather the datasets—which could come from several sources—needed to create the predictive model. Data analysts prepare the gathered information for analysis. In this process of data analysis and massaging, the unstructured data is transformed into a structured format [86].

There are numerous statistical and machine learning techniques used in the predictive analytics process. Regression analysis and probability theory are the two most significant methods that are frequently employed in analytics. Using the example dataset and statistical and machine learning methods, a model is created during the predictive modeling phase. The model is implemented for regular forecasts and decision-making at the client's site following the completion of successful prediction testing.

With predictive analytics, we can navigate the path ahead with the foresight of data on our side. So, let's harness the power of predictive analytics and design a more certain and successful future.

86. Kumar, V. 2018. Predictive Analytics: A Review of Trends and Techniques. International Journal of Computer Applications 182(1):31-37, DOI: 10.5120/ijca2018917434.

3.4 Prescriptive Analytics

When we leapfrog from the familiar ground of descriptive, inferential, and predictive analytics, we touch the less charted territory of prescriptive analytics. While the former types give us a "rearview mirror" perspective of what happened and why, or what could happen, prescriptive analytics is our magic compass, guiding us to the best future decisions[87].

Fundamentally, prescriptive analytics is selecting the best option or result from a range of options based on already-known parameters. Just think of it as a wise old sage, providing you with advice on how to maneuver through life's complex challenges based on knowledge, foresight, and wisdom. But instead of using life experience, this sage employs powerful algorithms and machine learning.

From healthcare to supply chain management, prescriptive analytics is leaving its footprints. In healthcare, it transforms the "one-size-fits-all" medical decision-making model, offering proactive decisions tailored to individual patients' needs[88]. In business, it helps predict and mitigate risks, optimize resources, and enhance customer satisfaction, ensuring better decision-making and business performance improvement[89].

---

87. Lepenioti, K., Bousdekis, A., Apostolou, D., Mentzas, G. 2020. Prescriptive analytics: Literature review and research challenges. International Journal of Information Management. Volume 50, February 2020, Pages 57-70.

88. Mosavi, N.S., Santos, M.F. 2020. How Prescriptive Analytics Influences Decision Making in Precision Medicine. Procedia Computer Science. Volume 177, 2020, Pages 528-533. https://doi.org/10.1016/j.procs.2020.10.073 .

89. Poornima, S., Pushpalatha, M. 2020. A survey on various applications of prescriptive analytics. International Journal of Intelligent Networks, Volume 1, 2020, Pages 76-84.

Digging a little deeper, we can imagine prescriptive analytics as a three-step ladder. At the first rung, we have the design of the system. This involves modeling real-world problems into a computational framework. Then, we ascend to the second rung, where we develop alternatives to transform possibilities into viable options[90]. Climbing to the final rung, we generate decision sets using sophisticated evolutionary algorithms to convert options into solutions, and then execute these decisions for real-world impact.

As magical as it sounds, achieving prescriptive analytics mastery requires patience and hard work. It won't happen at the push of a button. Organizations must go through the stages of descriptive, inferential, and predictive analytics and mature through them before they can reach this stage.

Company executives must take the lead to drive initiatives and recognize the benefits of prescriptive analytics. Prescriptive efforts may be avoided by many because they think the IT department should be in charge of them, because they are too complicated to show an acceptable return on investment (ROI), or because they think other sophisticated analytics projects should come first. But those who take the initiative to properly educate themselves on the category will be the ones who succeed[91].

90. Milchman, A., Fang, N. 2018. Prescriptive Analytics: A Short Introduction to Counterintuitive Intelligence. CreateSpace Independent Publishing Platform, 2018, ISBN: 197992970X, 9781979929707.

91. Bull, P., Centurion, C., Keams, S., Kelso, E. Viswanathan, N. 2017. Prescriptive Analytics for Business Leaders. Independent Publisher. ISBN: 1532357540, 9781532357541.

Heuristics (rules) and **exact algorithms** are the two types of algorithms available in the prescriptive analytics sector.[92]

Heuristics are approaches to problem-solving that can usually find a workable, reasonably good solution quite rapidly. The heuristics are empirically examined, and conclusions regarding the heuristic's quality can be drawn from these studies. Due to their speed and capacity for handling huge cases, heuristics are frequently employed in the solution of real-world issues[93]. The best solution is not always guaranteed by heuristic algorithms. When properly constructed, they can provide a quick and efficient way to locate quality solutions in a fair amount of time.

Exact algorithms ensure that the optimal answer is obtained. Such exact methods need to employ more advanced strategies. On the other hand, for challenging situations, the time required to find the optimal solution may grow exponentially in relation to the problem's size.

Any method intended to determine the optimal solution (optimization) needs to make use of a computer algorithm built upon a tried-and-true scientific methodology. The same mathematical proof is not necessary for a technique (heuristics) that is solely focused on locating a good answer. It's impossible to determine if a given heuristic would get the best result.

Prescriptive analytics solutions have to rely on rules or optimization by definition. While less frequent, it is conceivable

92. Kumar, V. 2018. Predictive Analytics: A Review of Trends and Techniques. International Journal of Computer Applications 182(1):31-37, DOI: 10.5120/ijca2018917434.

93. Ropke, S. 2005. Heuristic and exact algorithms for vehicle routing problems. Ph.D Thesis, Department of Computer Science at the University of Copenhagen (DIKU). Available at: https://www.researchgate.net/publication/200622125_Heuristic_and_exact_algorithms_for_vehicle_routing_problems .

for a prescriptive analytics solution to use both at the same time. Although there isn't always a better strategy than another, analysts and corporate executives need to know when to use each kind of approach (or both)[94].

Heuristics are rules that vary depending on the problem. When the issue can be precisely defined and is operational in nature as opposed to tactical or strategic, that is when they work best. They may also be a wise option when the same choices need to be made hundreds, thousands, or even millions of times every day. Heuristics make use of extremely specialized methods created to capitalize on certain features of an issue. Typically, they demand the creation of a series of instructions (such as "If this, then do this"), a set of mathematical functions (such as $f(x) = y$), or both.[95]

A popular tool for commercial decision-making is Excel. A hypothesis about a possible response can be used to construct Excel-based rules by utilizing features such as IF statements, lookups, and functions. After values are entered, the response is then given back right away. If an optimization method is not applied, there is no way to determine whether this is the optimal response.

Examples of situations when rules of thumb suffice and optimization is not necessary include:

- **Raw material purchases:** for example, buy raw materials from the lowest cost source first, regardless of quality;

94. Bull, P., Centurion, C., Keams, S., Kelso, E. Viswanathan, N. 2017. Prescriptive Analytics for Business Leaders. Independent Publisher. ISBN: 1532357540, 9781532357541.

95. Kumar, V. 2018. Predictive Analytics: A Review of Trends and Techniques. International Journal of Computer Applications 182(1):31-37, DOI: 10.5120/ijca2018917434.

- **Marketing:** provide consumers with promotional offers in response to their previous purchases or internet searches, for example;

- **Demand fulfillment:** for example, Tier 1 clients must always have their service requirements satisfied at the expense of those in other tiers.

To identify the best solution, optimization is used, which combines precise algorithms with mathematical modeling. Writing math equations on a model-building platform defines an issue. After the model is constructed, the problem is solved by a highly sophisticated algorithm. An aim must be specified to either maximize or minimize a metric (such as profit, costs, employee utilization, or volume) to get the best possible response.[96] The customer has the option to indicate how exactly they need the response to be as well as how long they can wait. The best response is then determined by the optimization algorithm.

In the past, optimization was used to tackle challenges related to a particular business function such as:

- **Transportation:** moving items at the lowest possible cost from supply to demand locations;

- **Equipment replacement:** figuring out when to replace equipment;

- **Assignment problems:** allocating workers to equipment;

- **Gasoline blending:** for aviation fuels[97].

96. Kumar, V. 2018. Predictive Analytics: A Review of Trends and Techniques. International Journal of Computer Applications 182(1):31-37, DOI: 10.5120/ ijca2018917434.

97. Bull, P., Centurion, C., Keams, S., Kelso, E. Viswanathan, N. 2017. Prescriptive Analytics for Business Leaders. Independent Publisher. ISBN: 1532357540, 9781532357541.

Prescriptive analytics is not just the future of big data - it's the "here and now" of effective decision-making. It's the key to unlocking new dimensions of growth, creating a bridge between the present and a plethora of optimized future possibilities. With prescriptive analytics, the future isn't something that just happens. It's something you shape, today.

Quiz

1. **What is the primary function of descriptive analytics?**

   a. To predict future trends

   b. To prescribe solutions to future problems

   c. To provide insights into future events

   d. To transform raw data into useful insights about past events

2. **Which of the following is an application of descriptive analytics in business?**

   a. To inform strategies and drive decision-making

   b. To replace other types of data analysis

   c. To solely review past events without context

   d. To be the only tool used in decision-making

3. **What are some techniques that descriptive analytics employs?**

   a. Data mining and clustering

   b. Data extraction and organization

   c. Data visualization and tabulation

   d. Data encryption and decryption

4. **Which statement best describes the flexibility of descriptive analytics?**

   a. It is restricted to specific industries.

   b. It can only be used by business leaders and scientists.

   c. It can be used in any industry and by every company.

   d. It is limited to large organizations with vast data resources.

5. **What does descriptive analytics provide for other types of data analysis techniques?**

   a. A competitive edge

   b. A stage for prescriptive analytics only

   c. The context and starting point

   d. A final verdict on data interpretation

6. **What is inferential analytics also known as?**

   a. Descriptive analytics

   b. Predictive analytics

   c. Inferential statistics

   d. Computational statistics

7. **Which of the following best describes the purpose of inferential analytics?**

   a. To merely describe the data in front of us

   b. To make educated predictions about larger data sets based on a smaller sample

   c. To predict tomorrow's weather

   d. To calculate the mean of a dataset

8. **Why is the use of sample data considered essential in inferential analytics?**

   a. It's more complicated and time-consuming

   b. It's simpler, less time-consuming, and more cost-effective

   c. It increases the chances of errors

   d. All of the above

9. **What are the two main types of inferential errors?**

   a. Type X error and type Y error

   b. Type I error and type II error

   c. Type A error and type B error

   d. Type 1 error and type 2 error

10. **What is the main difference between descriptive statistics and inferential statistics?**

   a. Descriptive statistics describes the data, while inferential statistics makes predictions about the data.

   b. Descriptive statistics uses probability, while inferential statistics does not.

   c. Descriptive statistics uses a sample, while inferential statistics uses the entire population.

   d. Descriptive statistics are more accurate than inferential statistics.

Answers	1 – d	2 – a	3 – a	4 – c	5 – c
	6 – c	7 – b	8 – b	9 – b	10 – a

Chapter Summary

Data analytics enables businesses to draw meaningful insights from collected data, facilitating smarter, data-driven decisions. There are four main types of data analytics: descriptive, inferential, predictive, and prescriptive:

◆ Descriptive analytics, the most used form, focuses on what has happened within a business, transforming historical data into easily understood information.

◆ Inferential analytics aims to determine why something occurred. This kind of analysis offers perceptions of the elements that contributed to a specific outcome by looking at correlations and relationships between various data points.

◆ Predictive analytics, on the other hand, concentrates on what might occur in the future. It forecasts upcoming occurrences using statistical models and forecasting methods based on past and present data. For risk reduction and proactive decision-making, this kind of analytics is essential.

◆ Prescriptive analytics offers insights into the course of action that should be followed to attain specific goals. It offers many decision possibilities and illustrates the effects of each choice. By outlining the most advantageous course of action to adopt, it goes beyond forecasting future results.

The appropriate use of these data analytic types helps businesses optimize their operations, make more informed decisions, and better meet their objectives.

Chapter 4

Techniques and Tools for Data Analytics

Organizations may improve their decision-making process, increase operational efficiency, and get a competitive edge in the market by utilizing the latest techniques, tools, and practices available in data analytics. However, because data analytics is a dynamically evolving field and therefore firms must constantly adapt their approach. This chapter will analyze what techniques and tools can we implement in data analytics and what are the best practices that can be incorporated.

The key learning objectives of this chapter are to dive into the details of the following topics:

- Data analytics techniques (regression analysis, exploratory data analysis, dimensional reduction techniques, machine learning algorithms, advanced analytics techniques)

- Data analytics tools (Excel, R, Python, SQL, RapidMiner, Hadoop, Apache Spark, Microsoft Power BI, Tableau, Qlik Sense, scikit-learn, and KNIME)

- The best practices in data analytics, that is, the three phases of workflow, reproducibility, regular data updates, data quality management, business-driven decisions, workflow integration, continuous learning, and adaptation.

4.1 Data Analytics Techniques

More than ever, the world is currently experiencing a data revolution that has an impact on almost every area of our everyday lives[98]. This data can be used to make better decisions, but we need the right tools to analyze it. Regression analysis and other statistical data analytics techniques can help us make sense of data and find insights.

Regression analysis

Regression analysis is a statistical technique that can be used to find the relationship between two or more variables. For example, we could use regression analysis to find the relationship between sales and marketing spend. Assume you're a sales manager attempting to forecast the sales figures for the upcoming month. Regression analysis can assist you in identifying the most

---

98. Sarker, I.H. 2021. Data Science and Analytics: An Overview from Data-Driven Smart Computing, Decision-Making and Applications Perspective. SN COMPUT. SCI. 2, 377 (2021). https://doi.org/10.1007/s42979-021-00765-8.

important factors, such as the weather or competitor promotion, that could have an impact on these numbers[99].

A popular type of regression analysis called **linear regression** is a statistical technique that is used to predict the value of a dependent variable (y) based on the value of one or more independent variables (x). The independent variables are those variables that are not dependent on other ones. They can also be the factors that are manipulated or controlled by the researcher in an experiment. The dependent variable is the outcome or result that researchers are interested in understanding or explaining.

Let's visualize a straightforward real-world scenario to simplify the idea of linear regression. Let's say you run a lemonade stand and you're curious about how the weather affects your sales each day. Since your sales are influenced by other variables, such as the weather, your weekly sales (let's use the number of cups of lemonade you sell) are what we refer to as the dependent variable in this case. Since the temperature fluctuates on its own and you're attempting to determine whether those variations have an impact on your sales, in this instance, it qualifies as an independent variable.

Attempting to create a straight line across a scatter of graph points (Figure 4.1)—each representing a day's temperature and associated lemonade sales—is what linear regression is all about. You want this line to accurately illustrate how temperature affects your sales as much as possible. "Best" means that the line should be as near to each of these places as it can be at the same time. Because real life isn't often that neat, it's uncommon to find a line that precisely crosses through every point.

99. Gallo, A. 2015. A Refresher on Regression Analysis. Harvard Business Review. URL: https://hbr.org/2015/11/a-refresher-on-regression-analysis.

Figure 4.1   **A visual explanation of regression analysis**

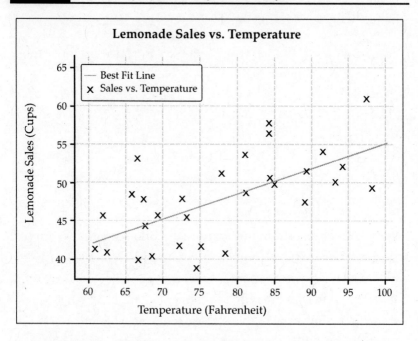

Individual data points, each reflecting a day's temperature (in Fahrenheit) and the matching quantity of lemonade sold, are displayed in the scatter plot. The best-fit line determined using linear regression is represented by the red line, which aims to show how temperature variations impact lemonade sales. This line aims to provide a general trend of increased sales with rising temperatures by minimizing the distance to all the data points at the same time. With the use of a straight line that best fits the data points, we attempt to predict the link between an independent variable (temperature) and a dependent variable (sales) in linear regression, as this example illustrates.

There are many other data analytics techniques besides regression analysis. Some of these techniques are described below.

Exploratory data analysis (EDA)

EDA is used to visualize and summarize data to get a better understanding of it. It is a crucial first step that prepares the data for more intricate studies, including visualizing, summarizing, and interpreting the data. EDA is often used before more formal data analysis techniques, as it can help us identify patterns and outliers in the data[100]. The term was coined by American mathematician John Wilder Tukey in the 1970s[101]. EDA aids in pattern recognition, outlier detection, hypothesis testing, and general data understanding[102]. Some examples are calculating the average income and standard deviation of incomes in a survey dataset to understand income distribution or a histogram of customer ages in a retail store dataset to analyze the age distribution and identify the store's primary customer age group.

Dimensional reduction techniques

Dimensional reduction techniques are used to reduce the number of variables in a dataset. This can be helpful when working with large datasets, as it can make the data easier to manage and analyze. By lowering the dimensionality of the data and condensing the data into fewer, easier to understand combinations of variables, techniques like Principal Component Analysis (PCA) aid in the simplification of this[103]. The Dimensional

---

100. Cham. 2016. Secondary Analysis of Electronic Health Records. MIT Critical Data. Springer, ISBN-13: 978-3-319-43740-8ISBN-13: 978-3-319-43742-2.

101. Dodge, Y. 2010. The concise Encyclopedia of Statistics. Springer, New York, NY. https://doi.org/10.1007/978-0-387-32833-1_136.

102. EPA. 2023. Exploratory Data Analysis. United States Environmental Protection Agency. URL: https://www.epa.gov/caddis-vol4/exploratory-data-analysis.

103. Rimal, Y. 2020. Regression Analysis of Large Research Data: Dimensional Reduction Techniques. In: Dawn, S., Balas, V., Esposito, A., Gope, S. (eds) Intelligent Techniques and Applications in Science and Technology. ICIMSAT 2019. Learning and Analytics in Intelligent Systems, vol 12. Springer, Cham. https://doi.org/10.1007/978-3-030-42363-6_35 .

Reduction Techniques improve model accuracy[104].

Customer segmentation for marketing objectives is a real-world application of dimensionality reduction techniques. Imagine a large retail company that gathers a lot of information about its customers: demographics (age, gender, income level), purchasing patterns (product preferences, purchase history, frequency of purchases), and engagement metrics (interactions on social media, website visits, and newsletter engagement). To better customize marketing strategies and enhance customer service, a deeper understanding of various client categories is the aim.

Using dimensionality reduction techniques might greatly aid in finding patterns and streamlining the analysis because of the high dimensionality and complexity of this dataset. The company can choose to employ Principal Component Analysis (PCA) to lower the dimensionality of the dataset. Principal components, a smaller group of uncorrelated variables, are created using PCA from the initial, potentially connected data. The arrangement of these elements ensures that the majority of the variety found in the original dataset is retained in the first few.

Machine learning algorithms

Machine learning algorithms are used to learn from data and make predictions. Machine learning algorithms can be used for a variety of tasks, such as fraud detection, customer segmentation, and product recommendations.

For example, many of today's most cutting-edge technologies, from Netflix's personalized recommendations to autonomous

---

104. Vachharajani, B. and Pandya, D. 2022. Dimension reduction techniques: Current status and perspectives. Proceedings to the International Conference on Additive Manufacturing and Advanced Materials (AM2). Volume 62, Part 13, pages 6913-7340 (2022).

automobiles, are powered by machine learning algorithms[105]. These algorithms provide computers the ability to see patterns in data and learn and make predictions. Like how humans learn from our past acts, they acquire new skills through experience without the necessity for explicit programming.

Regression can be considered a form of machine learning algorithm, but other methods like decision trees, random forests, and neural networks have become more well-liked.

Machine learning algorithms can be broadly divided into three groups: reinforcement learning (training method based on rewarding desired behaviors and/or punishing undesired ones), unsupervised learning, and supervised learning.

For example, labeled datasets are used to train supervised learning algorithms, which are ideal for tasks like forecasting stock market movements or categorizing emails as spam or not. On the other hand, unsupervised learning algorithms find patterns in unlabeled data that help group related things or spot anomalies.

105. Brown, S. 2021. Machine learning, explained. MIT Management Sloan School. URL: https://mitsloan.mit.edu/ideas-made-to-matter/machine-learning-explained .

Fun Fact

Did you know that the machine learning Random Forest method functions similarly to the Decision trees method and even better[106]? It appears as though a council of sage old trees from a fantastical book convened to make future predictions! Every tree in the "forest" gets to "vote" on the result after being trained on arbitrary data segments. Decisions based on evidence are made through a democratic process!

Advanced analytics techniques

Advanced analytics techniques are used for more complex data analysis tasks. Some examples of advanced analytics techniques include sentiment analysis, network analysis, and time series analysis. For example, a company could use sentiment analysis to track customer sentiment towards its products or services on social media, a financial institution could use network analysis to identify influential people in the financial market and a government agency could use time series analysis to predict the demand for electricity in the coming months.

Organizations can use data analytics techniques to find patterns, spot anomalies, forecast trends, and make data-driven decisions[107]. The importance of these techniques will only grow as we continue to produce and gather more data. By mastering these techniques, we give ourselves the ability to transform unstructured data into insightful knowledge that will guide

106. Jehad, A., Rehanullah, K., Nasir, A. Imran, M. 2012. Random Forests and Decision Trees. IJCSI International Journal of Computer Science Issues, Vol. 9, Issue 5, No 3, September 2012. ISSN (Online): 1694-0814.

107. Sarker, I.H. 2021. Data Science and Analytics: An Overview from Data-Driven Smart Computing, Decision-Making and Applications Perspective. SN COMPUT. SCI. 2, 377 (2021). https://doi.org/10.1007/s42979-021-00765-8.

us through the complicated, data-driven worlds of today and tomorrow.

4.2 Data Analytics Tools

Data analytics is essential to make well-informed decisions, analyze massive amounts of data, and predict future trends. Given its significance, many data analytics tools have been created and improved to make this process easier[108].

Understanding data analytics and the right tools for the job is crucial. Large-scale dataset-based data analytics uncovers hidden patterns and supports business transformation. Organizations must understand how the tool will fit into their overall business objectives before implementing it. A lot of new tools are hitting the market, and other technologies are becoming less important, as a result of the constantly evolving needs of those who work in data analytics[109]. Besides Microsoft Excel, there are other popular tools like R, Python, SQL, RapidMiner, Hadoop, Apache Spark, Microsoft Power BI, Tableau, Qlik Sense, scikit-learn, and KNIME.

Data analytics software use a variety of research techniques to store, process, and extract insights from the provided datasets. Certain technologies are even doing well in terms of generating improved visualization and summary reports, which helps us obtain accurate results with minimal work.[110]

---

108. Srinivasa, K., Kurni, M. (2021). Tools for Learning Analytics. In: A Beginner's Guide to Learning Analytics. Advances in Analytics for Learning and Teaching. Springer, Cham. https://doi.org/10.1007/978-3-030-70258-8_5.

109. Bonthu, S., Bindu, K.H. 2017. Review of Leading Data Analytics Tools. International Journal of Engineering & Technology, 7 (3.31) (2017) 10-15.

110. Gallo, A. 2015. A Refresher on Regression Analysis. Harvard Business Review. URL: https://hbr.org/2015/11/a-refresher-on-regression-analysis.

Microsoft Excel is a common data analysis tool. It has graphing tools, automated computing capabilities, and spreadsheet operations that can manage and organize big data sets. Due to its widespread use, it is a necessary tool for everyone beginning their data journey.

Quick Tips

Learn how to use the Pivot Table in Excel for effective data analytics. Pivot Tables are an efficient way to quickly summarize massive datasets and identify patterns and trends[111]. After deciding on your data range, click "Insert Pivot Table." Next, move various fields by dragging and dropping them into the Rows, Columns, Values, and Filters sections. Grouping data, calculating, and filtering for certain insights are all simple to do. To ensure that your analysis is current, don't forget to reload your Pivot Table if the underlying data changes!

Apache Spark is another well-known tool for managing big data analytics. It provides fault tolerance for entire clusters and an implicit data parallel programming interface. The SAS (Statistical Analysis System) software suite is used for corporate intelligence, data management, multivariate analysis, advanced analytics, and predictive analytics.

Because of their extensive libraries for statistical analysis, data visualization, and machine learning, Python and R are two of the most popular programming languages used in data analytics. An environment for executing Python and R code is provided by the

111. Pan, D. 2015. Advanced Data Analysis: From Excel PivotTables to Microsoft Access. Proceedings of the Charleston Library Conference. DOI: http://dx.doi. org/10.5703/1288284315592.

open-source web application Jupyter Notebook, making it simpler to create and share documents with live code, equations, graphics, and narrative prose[112].

Since its debut in 1991, Python has gained significant popularity as a general-purpose programming language. Python is an approachable, simple-to-learn, robust, and quick programming language. Because it was created under an OSI-approved Open Source license, this language can be distributed and used freely by anyone, even businesses.

The licensing for Python is managed by the Python Software Foundation. Python Package Index, or PyPI, is the host of numerous third-party Python modules. Python's extensive library makes it a highly useful tool for performing data analytics.[113] Data analysts are gravitating towards Python. Spyder, PyCharm, Rodeo, Atom, and Jupyter notebook are a few of the top Python integrated development environments (IDEs) for data analytics. The Jupyter notebook serves as a presentation and teaching tool in addition to being an intuitive, interactive environment. In the same notebook, there is code and output that can be shared as PDFs and many other file formats, including latex.

R is another Open Source software application that is managed by the R Foundation for Statistical Computing and is created by volunteers for use by scientists, researchers, and data analysts. R is freely accessible through the GNU General Public License. Statisticians use it extensively, and there is an abundance of

112. Fangohr, H., Beg, M., Bergemann, M., Bondar, V. 2019. Data exploration and analysis with Jupyter notebooks. Proceedings of The 17th International Conference on Accelerator and Large Experimental Physics Control Systems, New York, NY, USA, DOI: 10.18429/JACoW-ICALEPCS2019-TUCPR02.
113. Gallo, A. 2015. A Refresher on Regression Analysis. Harvard Business Review. URL: https://hbr.org/2015/11/a-refresher-on-regression-analysis.

internet advice available. Polls, data-mining surveys, and literature reviews on databases all indicate that R's popularity has skyrocketed in recent years. The 40-year SAS language monopoly has been challenged by the creation and application of R. Fortran, C, and R are used in the development of the R software environment. R offers a user-friendly command line interface, and all of its commands are simple to use and comprehend. These days, there are several graphical front-ends accessible, such as Rstudio, IntelliJ, Visual Studio, etc[114].

Microsoft Power BI and Tableau are at the top of the heap in the field of data visualization. With the help of Power BI, users can construct powerful, dynamic data representations from a range of sources, effectively conveying crucial business insights[115]. Microsoft Power-BI provides self-service BI competencies with interactive visualizations so staff members may generate dashboards and reports without assistance from the software development team[116].

The interface of Tableau, on the other hand, is straightforward enough for users to build their own dashboards, and it offers interactive visuals. Tableau allows you to connect to cloud-based data sources (such as big data, spreadsheets, SQL, Google Analytics, and Salesforce), do calculations using pre-existing data, produce forecasts and reference lines, and perform statistical

114. Bonthu, S., Bindu, K.H. 2017. Review of Leading Data Analytics Tools. International Journal of Engineering & Technology, 7 (3.31) (2017) 10-15.

115. Shoaib, G., Nandi, S. 2022. Power Bi Dashboard for Data Analysis. International Research Journal of Engineering and Technology (IRJET), Volume 09, Issue 07. e-ISSN: 2395-0056.

116. Dutta, P. 2019. Business Analytics using Microsoft Power BI and AWS Redshift. International Journal of Trend in Scientific Research and Development (IJTSRD), Volume: 3 | Issue: 2 | Jan-Feb 2019 Available Online: www.ijtsrd.com e-ISSN: 2456 - 6470.

summaries for trend analysis, regressions, and correlations. Users of this software can split, pivot, and manipulate metadata to optimize data sources without having to write any code[117].

Qlik Sense stands out among machine learning applications thanks to its associative analytics engine, cognitive features, and sturdy, scalable platform. It enables automated machine learning and intuitive data exploration. With Qlik Sense, data can be loaded without the need to manually update scripts, and the user interface may be simplified with drag-and-drop visualizations. The business intelligence tool for converting data into knowledge is called QlikView. Users can obtain unexpected business insights regarding the relationships between different types of data. Users can do both direct and indirect searches for overall data in any field or across the entire application[118].

With Qlik, you can include Google Analytics data into your research with ease[119]:

- Flexibility in combining data sources: Qlik's associative architecture allows for the smooth integration of data from social networking platforms, Google Analytics, and a few other data sources into data applications.

- Quick deployment: With the Qlik Google Analytics Connector, new insights can be obtained in a matter of

---

117. Salgador, J.P.Z. 2018. Data Analytics with Tableau: The Trend Lines Models. SSRN Electronic Journal, DOI:10.2139/ssrn.3282727.

118. Ghosh, S., Neha, K. 2019. Social Media Analytics using Qlik Connectors. International Journal of Recent Technology and Engineering (IJRTE). ISSN: 2277-3878, Volume-8, Issue-2S11, September 2019.

119. Ghosh, S., Neha, K. 2019. Social Media Analytics using Qlik Connectors. International Journal of Recent Technology and Engineering (IJRTE). ISSN: 2277-3878, Volume-8, Issue-2S11, September 2019.

hours rather than weeks or months. It is simple to configure and put into production.

- See every one of your websites in one location - It can be challenging to get a whole picture from a single perspective, particularly when we are comparing websites side by side. You may view everything in one location and choose the KPIs that are essential to you by hand with Qlik. Eliminate time-wasting transitions between website profiles and charts.

KNIME is a different program that integrates machine learning and data mining components and has a graphical interface for building data workflows. KNIME is currently among the top analytics systems for data breakthroughs that identify perhaps hidden patterns, mine for fresh insights, or forecast new features. Each of its thousands of modules includes a large selection of algorithms, hundreds of ready-to-run sample scripts, and a sufficient number of integrated tools. This utility integrates components using the modular pipelining idea.

Even novice users can use KNIME because all they have to do is drag and drop connecting points between activities. KNIME's drawbacks include its poor visualization, inability to handle complicated and large-scale workflows, inability to split many data sets, lack of wrapper methods, limited error measurement methods, and unavailability of preliminary results.

The majority of top tools offer Command Line Interface, which is a feature that most programmers find convenient. Table 4.1 lists the main features, including the current version, support for the command line, license, language in which they were produced, and functionality of certain software tools.

Table 4.1		General characteristics of the tools			
Tool	GUI/ CLI	Current version	License	Languyage used for development	Functionality
R	Both	3.3.3	GNU GPL v2	C. Fortran, R	Statistical Techniques
Python	Both	3.6.1.rcl	Python software foundation license	C, Python	General purpose programming
Rapid Miner	GUI	7.4	Profession edition is properietary, basic edition is AGPL	Java	Business Intellience, Machine Learning, predictive analytics
Hadoop	Both	3.0.0 alpha 2	Apache License 2.0	Java	Distributed environment
Spark	Both	2.1.0	Apache License 2.0	Scala, Java, Python, R	Data Analytics, Machine Learning
Tableau	GUI	10.1	Commercial	C++	Data Visualization
KNIME	GUI	3.3.1	GNU general public	Java	Data Analysis, Text Mining

Source: Bonthu, S., Bindu, K.H. 2017. Review of Leading Data Analytics Tools. International Journal of Engineering & Technology, 7 (3.31) (2017) 10-15.

Data analytics can be carried out on a variety of platforms, including the web, iPhones, and Android and Windows Phone mobile applications. Table 4.2 provides a comprehensive overview of which tool is compatible with which platform. Python is compatible with all platforms, although Windows phone apps cannot use R, Spark, Tableau, or KNIME. Hadoop is not compatible with all systems because it is a distributed environment.

Table 4.2	**Supported platforms**			
Tool	**Web**	**I-phone**	**Android**	**Windows phone**
R	✓	✓	✓	
Python	✓	✓	✓	✓
RapidMiner	✓			
Hadoop	✓			
Spark	✓	✓	✓	
Tableau	✓	✓	✓	
KNIME	✓	✓	✓	

Source: Bonthu, S., Bindu, K.H. 2017. Review of Leading Data Analytics Tools. International Journal of Engineering & Technology, 7 (3.31) (2017) 10-15.

The choice of a data analytics tool is influenced by the needs of the task at hand, the readily available infrastructure, and the user's expertise. Successful data analytics depend on having a solid understanding of these tools and how they are used[120].

4.3 Best Practices

The systematic examination of data, which results in informed decision-making, is a critical step in data analytics. Any data analytics project must have a well-organized and efficient workflow to be successful. Here are some guidelines for designing a data analytics pipeline: three phases of workflow, reproducibility, regular data updates, data quality management,

---

120. Stoudt, S., Vasquez, V.N., Martinez, C.C. 2021. Principles for data analysis workflows. PLOS Computational Biology. https://doi.org/10.1371/journal.pcbi.1008770

business-driven decisions, workflow integration, continuous learning, and adaptation.

Three phases of workflow: Explore, refine, and produce are the three stages of an efficient data analysis process, according to Stoudt et al [121]. The explore phase is focused on initial data investigation, comprehension, and hypothesis formation. In the refine phase, raw data are converted into a format that can be analyzed and used to explore models or statistical techniques. Producing the final analysis and figures, and writing up the findings are all part of the produce phase.

Reproducibility: Workflows for data analysis must be able to be replicated. This entails making sure that other people can accurately reproduce the actions made during the workflow. It improves the findings' dependability and openness. Tools like R Markdown or Jupyter Notebook, which enable the combination of code, output, and descriptive text, can be helpful in this situation[122].

Regular data updates: It's critical to design a procedure that allows managing new data and rerunning studies with the updated data for datasets that are often updated[123]. This process can be streamlined by using automation technologies.

Data quality management: Ensuring the accuracy and reliability of the data is a critical step in the data analytics workflow.

121. Stoudt, S., Vásquez, V.N., Martinez, C.C. 2021. Principles for data analysis workflows. PLoS Comput Biol 17(3): e1008770. https://doi.org/10.1371/journal.pcbi.1008770 .

122. Wratten, L., Wilm, A. & Göke, J. 2021. Reproducible, scalable, and shareable analysis pipelines with bioinformatics workflow managers. Nat Methods 18, 1161–1168 (2021). https://doi.org/10.1038/s41592-021-01254-9 .

123. Yenni, G.M., Christensen, E.M., Bledsoe, E.K., Supp, S.R., Diaz, R.M., White, E.P., et al. 2019. Developing a modern data workflow for regularly updated data. PLoS Biol 17(1): e3000125. https://doi.org/10.1371/journal.pbio.3000125 .

Results can be misled by inconsistent, inaccurate, or missing data. To address these challenges, the pipeline should include data cleaning and validation procedures.

Business-driven decisions: The goal of data analytics is to address practical issues and provide information to support business choices. Therefore, the choice of which business issues to concentrate on should be made jointly by business leaders and data scientists. The data and analytics capabilities ought to correspond to the particular business requirements[124].

Workflow integration: Data science cannot be done in a vacuum. It needs to be thoroughly integrated into organizational structure, business processes, and operations[125]. This necessitates ongoing interaction and coordination between the various parties participating in the workflow of data analysis.

To improve customer support, an e-commerce company can integrate data analytics with its customer service workflow. Their solution gives support workers instant access to purchase history, stock information, and supply chain specifics by connecting client interactions with inventory data. Sentiment analysis uses the customer's tone to infer satisfaction and urgency, enabling customized answers like coupons, quick returns, or different suggestions. Response times, client satisfaction, and inventory forecasts are all enhanced by this integration.

124. Mayor, T. 2023. How to build an effective analytics practice: 7 insights from MIT experts. MIT Management Sloan School. URL: https://mitsloan.mit.edu/ideas-made-to-matter/how-to-build-effective-analytics-practice-7-insights-mit-experts .

125. O'Toole, T. 2020. What's the Best Approach to Data Analytics? Harvard Business Review. URL: https://hbr.org/2020/03/whats-the-best-approach-to-data-analytics .

Continuous learning and adaptation: Because data analytics tools and techniques are developing so quickly, a portion of the workflow should be set aside for learning and applying these new methods. This will guarantee that the workflow remains efficient and current.

By adhering to these best practices, businesses can make sure that their workflow for data analytics is scalable, reproducible, and in line with their corporate goals in addition to being successful at extracting important insights from data.[126]

126. Yenni, G.M., Christensen, E.M., Bledsoe, E.K., Supp, S.R., Diaz, R.M., White, E.P., et al. 2019. Developing a modern data workflow for regularly updated data. PLoS Biol 17(1): e3000125. https://doi.org/10.1371/journal.pbio.3000125.

Quiz

1. **What is the purpose of regression analysis in data analytics?**

   a. To measure the correlation between a dependent variable and one or more independent variables

   b. To predict future weather patterns

   c. To analyze the growth of a business over time

   d. To create data sets for further analysis

2. **Who coined the term exploratory data analysis (EDA) in the 1970s?**

   a. Albert Einstein

   b. John Wilder Tukey

   c. Alan Turing

   d. Isaac Newton

3. **What are the three broad categories into which machine learning algorithms can be divided?**

   a. Reinforcement learning, unsupervised learning, and supervised learning

   b. Active learning, passive learning, and supervised learning

   c. Reinforcement learning, unsupervised learning, and dynamic learning

   d. Active learning, unsupervised learning, and static learning

4. **What is a notable assumption of linear regression analysis?**

   a. The residuals are constant across observations.

   b. The residuals are different across observations.

   c. The dependent and independent variables have a non-linear relationship.

   d. There is no correlation between the dependent and independent variables.

5. **What is the purpose of dimensional reduction techniques in data analytics?**

   a. To improve the accuracy of data models

   b. To increase the complexity of data sets

   c. To enhance the speed of data processing

   d. To increase the dimensionality of data

6. **Why is data analytics essential?**

   a. To analyze large amounts of data

   b. To make well-informed decisions

   c. To predict future trends

   d. All of the above

96

7. **What is a common feature of Microsoft Excel used in data analytics?**

    a. Graphing tools

    b. Spreadsheet operations

    c. Automated computing capabilities

    d. All of the above

8. **Which programming languages are popular in data analytics due to their extensive libraries for statistical analysis, data visualization, and machine learning?**

    a. Python and JavaScript

    b. Java and R

    c. Python and R

    d. JavaScript and Java

9. **Which software is known for advanced analytics, multivariate analyses, corporate intelligence, data management, and predictive analytics?**

    a. Apache Spark

    b. SAS (Statistical Analysis System)

    c. Microsoft Power BI

    d. Tableau

10. What is a unique feature of Qlik Sense in the field of data analytics?

   a. Robust, scalable platform

   b. Associative analytics engine

   c. Cognitive features

   d. All of the above

Answers	1 – a	2 – b	3 – a	4 – a	5 – a
	6 – d	7 – d	8 – c	9 – b	10 – d

Chapter Summary

◆ As the complexity and diversity of data increase, a broad range of techniques are developed to accommodate them. Some of the most known techniques include regression analysis, exploratory regression analysis, dimensional reduction techniques, machine learning algorithms, and advanced analytics.

◆ There are various tools used in data analytics that are critical in processing massive amounts of data and have been continuously improved and innovated to simplify this process. The most common are Microsoft Excel, Python and R, Apache Spark, Microsoft Power BI, and Tableau.

◆ The best practices in data analytics are to respect the three phases of the workflow scheme, reproducibility, regular data updates, data quality management, business-driven decisions, workflow integration, and continuous learning and adaptation.

Chapter **5**

What Does a Data Analyst Do?

So, what exactly does a data analyst do? What procedures do data analytics involve? This chapter will go into the data analytics process, which is the cornerstone of data-driven decision-making. Data analytics essentially consists of five stages: identifying the questions, collecting the data, cleaning the data, analyzing the data, and ultimately visualizing and sharing the results.

The key learning objectives of this chapter include the reader's understanding of the following:

- The data analytics process and the steps necessary to complete a data analyst's job

- Defining the questions for conducting the data analysis process

- Collecting data, that is, gathering pertinent facts to address the issue

- Cleaning the data, that is, correcting and eliminating flaws or inconsistencies in the data that has been gathered

- Analyzing the data to find patterns, trends, and insights

- Visualizing and sharing the findings: the final step entails communicating the insights with stakeholders by presenting the findings in a clear, aesthetically appealing way

Readers will be equipped to traverse the complex world of data analytics and use the power of data to propel effective decision-making by understanding these phases and the methodologies used in each.

5.1 The Data Analytics Process

Data analytics is a scientific method that involves examining raw data in order to make inferences about that information. Making educated judgments, forecasting future trends, and improving an organization's overall operational efficiency are all achieved through this complex process, which applies a variety of methodologies from several disciplines[127].

The data analytics process is an iterative one that includes several significant stages rather than a single step. The stages are:

127. Moreira, João Mendes, André C. P. L. F. de Carvalho, and Tomáš Horváth. 2019. A General Introduction to Data Analytics. John Wiley & Sons, Inc.

Defining the questions

Defining the goal or problem statement is the first stage in the data analytics process. The objective is to comprehend what kinds of insights the company hopes to obtain from the data analysis. This process entails formulating a specific question considering the requirements or objectives of the company.

Collecting data

Data analysts gather the essential information after formulating the problem statement. This information may come from a variety of sources, including consumer surveys, purchase records, social media activity, and more. The gathered information is essential for later analysis and meaningful conclusion-making.

Cleaning the data

The obtained data must be processed and cleaned before analysis can begin. This stage makes sure that irrelevant, incomplete, or incorrect data is eliminated, increasing the analysis's accuracy.

Analyzing the data

After the data has been prepared and cleansed, the analysis itself can begin. To find trends, patterns, and insightful information, several statistical and mathematical techniques are applied in this step. The analysis process may use a variety of methodologies, including prescriptive, diagnostic, predictive, and descriptive analytics.

Visualizing and sharing the findings

The results of the analysis are communicated to the necessary parties after completion. To facilitate simpler comprehension and faster decision-making, the data are frequently presented in a visually appealing fashion.

Since data analytics is an ongoing process, it is acceptable to fail and try again using a different strategy. Accepting failure can assist you in learning and refining the procedure to better suit your requirements.

Furthermore, corporate operations, processes, and organizational structure should be closely connected with good data analytics[128]. But it's crucial to keep in mind that this procedure is adaptable and can be changed in accordance with particular requirements and objectives.

Fun Fact

Less than 0.5% of the data we create is thought to be examined and used[129], which is an interesting fact about the data analytics process. This implies that while we are producing a huge ocean of data, we are only examining a small portion of it!

5.2 Defining the Questions

Any company or research project needs to start by defining the research questions. This step prepares the ground for an effective data exploration process and helps to reveal valuable and useful insights.

128. O'Toole, T. 2020. What's the Best Approach to Data Analytics? Harvard Business Review. URL: https://hbr.org/2020/03/whats-the-best-approach-to-data-analytics .

129. Gauld, A.. 2017. Insight Driven Organisation survey. Report: Benchmarking your analytics journey. Deloitte company report, 2017. Available at: https://www2.deloitte.com/content/dam/Deloitte/uk/Documents/technology/deloitte-uk-tech-ido-survey.pdf

It's critical to comprehend your data, its source, and its nature before defining the questions. For instance, big data has completely changed the field of scientific research and data analytics[130]. Understanding the context and possibilities of your data, whether it be genomic sequences, physiological measures, or information on traffic flow, can help you formulate targeted and relevant queries.

Generally speaking, the quality of your data depends on the questions you pose[131]. Specificity and alignment with the ultimate objective of your business or research undertaking are required of the questions. If you run a medical business, the inquiries can be intended to enhance customer relations or anticipate future medical needs. Your inquiries may concern bettering diagnosis and treatment or comprehending the nutritional requirements of a group in the context of scientific research.

Asking the appropriate questions is the secret. Engage in regular discussions with company executives, data scientists, and other pertinent stakeholders to identify these questions. Data analytics ought to be integrated into the company and coordinated with the operational procedures. These discussions may raise new issues, creative solutions, and unexpected opportunities that weren't previously thought about.

---

130. Stanford Edu. 2020. Scientific Research and Big Data. Stanford Encyclopedia of Philosophy. URL: https://plato.stanford.edu/entries/science-big-data/ .

131. McCord, S.E., Karl, J.W., Fults, G., Webb, N.P. 2021. Ten practical questions to improve data quality. Society for Range Management, Rangelands, RALA-00301, DOI: 10.1016/j.rala.2021.07.006.

Quick Tips

A quick tip is to use the SMART criteria (Specific, Measurable, Achievable, Relevant, and Time-bound) while defining questions in the data analytics process. You can more effectively concentrate your data analytics efforts and obtain useful insights by making sure your questions fit these requirements.

Data analytics questions may be descriptive, inferential, predictive, or prescriptive. For illustration, "What were the sales figures for the last quarter?" would be a descriptive inquiry. The following could be an inferential query: "Why did sales decline in the last quarter?" Advanced statistical modeling is needed to answer questions like "What will be our sales in the next quarter?" In order to make strategic decisions, prescriptive questions like "How can we improve sales next quarter?" draw on information from all three earlier question categories.

Information literacy, which refers to the capacity to locate, assess, and make efficient use of sources[132], is a key component of a comprehensive approach to question framing in data analytics. As the questions are established, it is important to assess the data sources and confirm their reliability.

In conclusion, properly structuring your questions considering the nature of your study, and doing a thorough assessment of your information sources are all essential components of developing questions in data analytics. At the core of successful data analytics is a methodical procedure that directs your investigation and analysis.

---

132. Sharma, S., Deepmala, Upadhyay, A.K. 2021. Information Literacy: An Overview. Ilkogretim Online - Elementary Education Online, 2021; Vol 20 (Issue 1): pp. 4227-4234. doi: 10.17051/ilkonline.2021.01.465

5.3 Collecting Data

The systematic process of gathering and measuring information on variables of interest, in a systematic manner, that enables answering the research questions, is known as data collection[133]. No matter if you are conducting research for commercial, governmental, or academic goals, data collecting gives you the chance to learn firsthand information and develop novel insights into your study issue.

Although the method for collecting data may differ between disciplines, the overall structure is typically similar. It is a sequential procedure that requires careful planning to guarantee the accuracy and dependability of your data.

You can primarily collect two different sorts of data: quantitative (numerical) and qualitative (non-numerical). You might require both sorts of data in the scenario of analyzing the sales trend on Christmas, from year to year. Quantitative data can include previous Christmas season sales figures, while qualitative data might include customer comments or surveys regarding shopping preferences.

Choosing the right procedures and methods you'll employ to acquire your data is very important. Data can be gathered using a variety of techniques, including surveys, interviews, observation, and the use of pre-existing information[134]. You must make a

---

133. Kabir, S.M.S. 2016. Methods of Data Collection. In book: Basic Guidelines for Research: An Introductory Approach for All Disciplines (pp.201-275). Publisher: Book Zone Publication.

134. Kabir, S.M.S. 2016. Methods of Data Collection. In book: Basic Guidelines for Research: An Introductory Approach for All Disciplines (pp.201-275). Publisher: Book Zone Publication.

reasonable decision depending on your research objective and the type of data you require because each method has benefits and drawbacks of its own.

For instance, you could use the retail company's historical sales data to gather quantitative information on sales. You might select to carry out surveys or interviews to gather qualitative information about client purchasing patterns.

 One interesting real-life example of data collection in data analytics is the "Smart Diapers" project developed by a startup. The "Smart Diapers" project involves a startup embedding sensor strips in baby diapers to track health indicators like hydration, kidney function, and infection risk[135]. A smartphone app analyzes the data and sends out real-time health alerts for the infant to parents and clinicians, enabling prompt medical attention to any abnormalities found.

Contemporary manufacturing is another area of interest for data collection. Data collectors, such as sensors, are tasked with capturing meaningful physical values produced by manufacturing events, as shown in Figure 5.1. In order to make the best decisions possible to improve the production system's performance, the collected data is further examined and analyzed. Unlike traditional model-based manufacturing, this closed-loop method of production established a foundational framework for data-driven manufacturing[136].

---

135. Prayaga, V. 2020. Smart Diapers. Research proposal. Research Gate, DOI: 10.13140/RG.2.2.29246.92480.

136. Xu, K., Li, Y., Liu, C., Liu, X., Hao, X., Gao, J., Maropoulos, P.G. 2020. Advanced Data Collection and Analysis in Data-Driven Manufacturing Process. Chinese Journal of Mechanical Engineering (2020) 33:43. https://doi.org/10.1186/s10033-020-00459-x.

Figure 5.1	Closing the loop of data-driven manufacturing

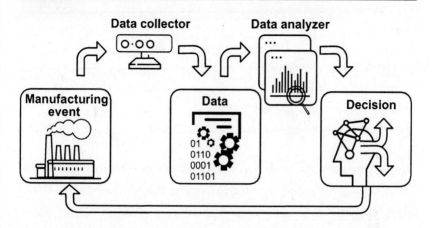

Source: Xu, K., Li, Y., Liu, C., Liu, X., Hao, X., Gao, J., Maropoulos, P.G. 2020. Advanced Data Collection and Analysis in Data-Driven Manufacturing Process. Chinese Journal of Mechanical Engineering (2020) 33:43. DOI: https://doi.org/10.1186/s10033-020-00459-x.

You need to think about your data processing and storage methods as well. The prevalence of digital data is growing, so it's critical to use effective and secure data storage techniques. Another important stage is converting raw data into a format that can be used. Also, keep in mind that collecting data is an iterative process. Based on the information you gather; you might need to review your plan and make adjustments. Data collection is an art unto itself. Your data analytics project is supported by a planned, organized approach. Spend the time necessary to collect the data accurately because it will serve as the basis for your analysis and insights. Throughout the process, keep your research goal in mind and make sure the information you gather is pertinent to and valuable for that goal.

5.4 Cleaning the Data

Data cleansing, sometimes referred to as data cleaning or data scrubbing[137], is one of the crucial phases in data analytics. The goal of this process is to identify potential data inconsistencies or flaws and fix them to improve the quality of your data.

When conducting quantitative research, we gather information and use statistical techniques to provide an answer to a particular research topic. We use hypothesis testing to see whether our data show support for our study hypotheses. However, handling data that has not been properly calibrated or cleansed can result in a variety of research biases[138], including information bias and bias due to omitted variables. To ensure that our data is legitimate, accurate, complete, consistent, unique, and uniform, it is crucial to clean it.

The process of data cleaning is done according to how the data is evaluated.

For businesses, poor data quality (DQ) is still a major problem. For the purposes of data warehousing and integration, data must be cleaned of mistakes in both structure and content. Since data cleansing is primarily concerned with data quality and getting the data fit for use by its users by eliminating errors and providing appropriate documentation, there is a great need for it. Several rounds of data auditing are used in current data cleaning methods

137. Rahm, E., Do, H.H. 2000. Data Cleaning: Problems and Current Approaches. Bulletin of the IEEE Computer Society Technical Committee on Data Engineering.

138. Ho, D.A., Beyan, O. 2020. Biases in Data Science Lifecycle. ArXiv. URL: https://arxiv.org/pdf/2009.09795.pdf .

to identify flaws and lengthy transformations are performed to correct them[139].

Numerous methods are employed for data cleansing in the manufacturing sector, educational institutions, universities, and other establishments. Long wait times are required of users, and they frequently create intricate transformation scripts. The most popular DC frameworks are examined in Table 5.1 to show their advantages and disadvantages. Among them are ARKTOS, AJAX, IntelliClean, and Potter's Wheel[140].

---

139. Sarpong, K.A-M., Arthur, J.K. 2013. Analysis of Data Cleansing Approaches regarding Dirty Data – A Comparative Study. International Journal of Computer Applications (0975 – 8887), Volume 76– No.7, August 2013.

140. Muller, H., Freytag, J.-C.. (2003). Problems, Methods, and Challenges in Comprehensive Data Cleansing. Journal of Computer Science, Humboldt-Univ. zu Berlin, 2005, pp. 21.

| Table 5.1 | Comparative analysis of data cleaning frameworks |

Parameter	Porters Wheel	AJAX	IntelliClean	ARKTOS
Interactivity	It is very interactive; hence easy to use	Complex interface and hence not friendly to non-technical persons.	Interactive with end user. However, requires little input from end-users	Highly interactive; it has graphical in terfaces for loading and executing validations on loaded files.
Data format/ Structure	Text	Text	Text	Text
Human dependency	High human dependency for exceptional errors.	High human dependency. Example; evaluation and validation of errors are fully dependent o human expert.	Very minimal because of the expert module embedded in the system.	Although the system has complex modules for dealing with duplicates, however, there is a high dependency on human expects for error correction.
Maintenance	Not considered	Not considered	Not considered	Not considered

Source: Sarpong, K.A-M., Arthur, J.K. 2013. Analysis of Data Cleansing Approaches regarding Dirty Data – A Comparative Study. International Journal of Computer Applications (0975 – 8887), Volume 76– No.7, August 2013.

Breaking the process of data cleaning into more detailed pieces, we can identify several aspects of data cleaning such as data validation, data screening, diagnosing phase, de-duplication, handling invalid data, dealing with missing data, or identifying outliers.

Data validation is the initial step in the data cleansing process. This phase involves determining whether the collected data adheres to the established formats and regulations. Oftentimes, in big organizations, data validation is done using statistical systems[141]. Any discrepancies discovered during this stage should be fixed right away. This could entail reformatting data, making changes to it, or eliminating it if it is useless.

Another key stage is **data screening**, which entails going over the data set to check for inconsistencies or inaccuracies. This may entail finding missing data, identifying outliers (unusual data values), or searching for incorrectly submitted data. Here, you need to have a keen eye and a comprehension of the data you're working with.

Data analysts discover all particular problems that require attention during the **diagnosing phase**[142]. For instance, we might discover that some measures don't accurately represent the values of the things being measured. Finding the right answers in this case requires understanding the type of errors.

---

141. Di Zio, M., Fursova, N., Gelsema, T., Gießing, S., Guarnera, U., Petrauskienė, J., Kalben, L.Q., Scanu, M., Bosch, K.O., van der Loo, M., Walsdorfer, K. 2016. Methodology for Data Validation 1.0. Essnet Validat Foundation. URL: https://cros-legacy.ec.europa.eu/system/files/methodology_for_data_validation_v1.0_rev-2016-06_final.pdf .

142. Van der Broeck, J., Herbst, A.J., Cunningham, S.A. 2005. Data Cleaning: Detecting, Diagnosing, and Editing Data Abnormalities. PLoS Medicine, Volume 2, Issue 10, DOI: 10.1371/journal.pmed.0020267.

Inconsistent conclusions can be drawn from your data analysis as a result of duplicate items in your dataset. **De-duplication** is thus one of the important processes in the data cleansing process[143]. This entails looking for, spotting, and eliminating duplicate records from your data set.

Data that does not adhere to the necessary format or values is considered invalid. Knowing how to **handle invalid data** is crucial. The invalid data could be the result of faulty data extraction techniques, system problems, or data entering issues. Depending on the situation, erroneous data may need to be deleted, corrected if the actual value is known, or estimated based on other data.

If a respondent might choose not to answer a question in a survey, data might not be gathered for that specific variable. Data may be lost due to technical problems. Different approaches to **dealing with missing data**, such as disregarding them, utilizing statistical methods to estimate the missing values, or using algorithms that can manage missing data, can be utilized depending on the type and extent of the missing data.

Data points known as outliers diverge greatly from other observations. They may appear as a result of errors or data variability. Extreme numbers on either the high or low end of a variable can be considered outliers. In some analyses, they can offer insightful information, but they can also bias the data and produce false findings. Data cleansing therefore includes locating outliers and managing them appropriately. Figure 5.2 gives an example of 3 outliers (marked as cases 1, 2, and 3).

---

143. Udechukwu, A., Ezeife, C., Barker, K. 2003. Independent De-duplication in Data Cleaning. Conference Proceedings for the 5th International Conference on Enterprise Information Systems (ICEIS) 2003.

Figure 5.2 **Various outlier examples from regression analysis. Case 1 is an anomaly concerning X. Case 2 is an anomaly in relation to Y. In terms of X and Y, Case 3 is an anomaly.**

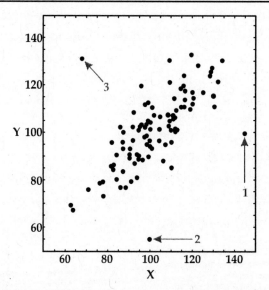

Source: Cousineau, D., Chartier, S. 2010. Outliers detection and treatment: a review. International Journal of Psychological Research, 3 (1), 59-68. ISSN: 2011-2084. DOI: 10.21500/20112084.844.

Your analysis and outcomes will be directly impacted by the quality of your data. Spending sufficient effort during the data cleansing step is thus not a loss of time but rather a worthwhile investment in the effectiveness of your investigation as a whole.

5.5 Analyzing the Data

Data analysis is a critical stage that occurs after the data has been prepared. It includes four key functional elements: descriptive, diagnostic, predictive, and prescriptive analytics. This multifaceted approach is crucial for providing a comprehensive view of data and making informed decisions.

To conduct an effective data analysis, it is crucial to select the appropriate data analytics techniques. This should be done based on the characteristics of the processed dataset, which are identified in the questions-defining stage[144]. There are many analytical techniques available, including, but not limited to, regression analysis, exploratory data analysis, dimensional reduction techniques, machine learning algorithms, and advanced analytics, as they were mentioned in previous sections of this book.

These techniques provide unique insights into the data but should be chosen carefully as each has its strengths and limitations. Selecting the right method involves considering the nature of the data and the specific objectives of the study. For example, if the objective is to predict a continuous value, regression would be the suitable choice. For instance, in a business context, it could be used to determine how changes in a marketing budget might impact sales.

Exploratory data analysis (EDA) is a foundational technique that can help to simplify high-dimensional data while retaining as much of the original information as possible. On the other hand, dimensional reduction techniques are particularly useful when dealing with complex machine learning models or large datasets[145].

Another technique is machine learning which allows us to go beyond the simple analysis of past and current data and venture into predictive analysis. For example, from the supervised machine learning models, linear regression, K-nearest neighbor,

144. Jajuga, K., Sokolowski, A., Bock, H.H. 2002. Classification, Clustering, and Data Analysis. Recent Advances and Applications. Conference Proceedings of The Eighth Conference of the International Federation of Classification Societies (IFCS), 2002.

145. Liu, M., Wang, Z., Gong, Z. 2020. Data Exploration. ML - CMU EDU. URL: https://blog.ml.cmu.edu/2020/08/31/2-data-exploration/ .

support vector regressor, and decision tree, can be employed to analyze financial accounting data, including balance sheets, income statements, and cash flow statement data[146]. These models helped in increasing profitability, maximizing performance, and cutting costs by finding more effective ways to run the firm.

Analyzing data is a complex process involving the application of various techniques and the choice of a technique depends on the nature of the data and the research objectives. Through proper interaction with the data, analysts can draw meaningful insights and make informed decisions.

5.6 Visualizing and Sharing the Findings

The data analytics process' crucial final steps include visualizing and sharing the findings. Utilizing these tactics can assist in communicating effectively and improving decision-making by assisting stakeholders in appreciating the value of the data.

To make complex data sets easier to grasp and analyze, data visualization is the activity of converting raw data into a graphical or pictorial format[147]. Data is "played" via visualization by providing an approachable, appealing format.

---

146. Chakri, P., Pratap, S., Lakshay, Gouda, S.K. 2023. An exploratory data analysis approach for analyzing financial accounting data using machine learning. Elsevier - Decision Analytics Journal, Volume 7, June 2023, 100212. https://doi.org/10.1016/j.dajour.2023.100212 .

147. Sadiku, M.N.O., Shadare, A.E., Musa, S.M., Akujuobo, C.M. 2016. Data Vizualization. International Journal of Engineering Research and Advanced Technologies (IJERAT), Volume 02, Issue 12, December 2016. ISSN: 2454-6135.

Understanding your message is the first step in producing good visualizations. The sort of visualization to use—idea illustration, idea generation, visual discovery, or everyday data visualization—is determined by this comprehension[148]. For instance, we might produce an "idea illustration" (the effective, efficient representation and communication of difficult ideas, concepts, or facts through the use of visual elements) if our goal is to make a declaration based on data-driven knowledge. On the other hand, "visual discovery" (utilizing interactive visual interfaces for data exploration and analysis) would be more appropriate if we were looking at data-driven information.

To support the data-driven decision-making process, the data must be successfully shared after they have been visualized. How you go about doing this greatly relies on how well-versed in data analytics your audience is. Visualizations can be very helpful in demystifying complex data sets for audiences with limited technical knowledge.

Effective transitions can help to show linkages between facts and data while sharing findings. These transitions aid readers in understanding data-driven conclusions. By bridging the gap between data specialists and business strategists, effective data analysis communication helps improve comprehension of the value produced by data.

However, even the most persuasive visualizations might fail to impress. One way to increase the probability of impressing the audience is by telling stories through visualizations. Analysts must consider the component of "data storytelling" as they communicate their findings. This idea entails contextualizing

148. Berinato, S. 2016. Visualizations That Really Work. Published in Harvard Business Review, June 2016: Managing the 24/7 Workplace.

the figures, telling a story with the facts, and emphasizing the insights. Following the example of the scientific picture word book, "1000 Words: Science: Build Knowledge, Vocabulary, and Literacy Skills (Vocabulary Builders),"[149] it is also essential to use terminology that non-technical stakeholders can understand.

The capacity to properly visualize and share discoveries is essential in a world where decision-making is becoming more and more dependent on data. Understanding these procedures will enable us to maximize the benefits of our data analytics efforts, resulting in strategic insights and well-informed judgments.

---

149. Pottle, J. 2021. 1000 Words: Science: Build Knowledge, Vocabulary, and Literacy Skills (Vocabulary Builders). Dorling Kindersley Limited.

Quiz

1. **Which of the following is the first stage in the data analytics process?**

   a. Collecting data

   b. Analyzing the data

   c. Visualizing and sharing the findings

   d. Defining the questions

2. **What type of data could be the sources for data analysts when collecting data?**

   a. Consumer surveys

   b. Purchase records

   c. Social media activity

   d. All of the above

3. **What is an acceptable approach when data analytics does not yield the desired results?**

   a. Stop the process and move to a different project.

   b. Stick to the current strategy and do nothing.

   c. Accept failure and try again using a different strategy.

   d. Hire a new data analyst.

4. **Why is defining research questions important for a company or research project?**

   a. To increase the budget of the project.

   b. To prepare the ground for an effective data exploration process and reveal useful insights.

   c. To create a hierarchy in the organization.

   d. To make the project more complicated.

5. **What are the types of data analytics questions that can be formulated?**

   a. Numeric, logical, and comparative

   b. Descriptive, inferential, predictive, and prescriptive

   c. Descriptive, philosophical, creative, and redundant

   d. Inferential, practical, redundant, and descriptive

6. **What does information literacy refer to in the context of data analytics?**

   a. The capacity to use computers and software

   b. The capacity to locate, assess, and make efficient use of sources

   c. The ability to write complex codes for data analysis

   d. The ability to present data in a visually appealing way

7. How does big data change the field of scientific research and data analytics?

a. By reducing the complexity of data

b. By limiting the amount of data for research

c. By changing the format of the data

d. By providing opportunities for deep data exploration and unveiling the hidden context and possibilities

8. Why is the quality of your data heavily dependent on the questions you pose?

a. Because the questions guide the data collection and analysis process

b. Because data itself poses questions

c. Because questions help in sorting the data

d. Because questions help in data encryption

9. What is data collection?

a. The process of gathering and measuring information on variables of interest in a systematic manner

b. The process of gathering any information

c. The process of measuring any information

d. None of the above

10. **What are the two main types of data that can be collected?**

   a. Inferred and implied data

   b. Direct and indirect data

   c. Quantitative (numerical) and qualitative (non-numerical) data

   d. Physical and virtual data

Answers	1 – d	2 – d	3 – c	4 – b	5 – b
	6 – b	7 – d	8 – a	9 – a	10 – c

Chapter Summary

◆ Data analytics involves a multi-step process that includes defining the problem, collecting relevant data, cleaning the data, analyzing it, and finally, visualizing and sharing the findings.

◆ This process helps to make educated judgments, predict future trends, and enhance an organization's overall operational efficiency.

◆ The first crucial step in any data analytics process is defining the research questions, which sets the stage for effective data exploration and extracting valuable insights. This requires understanding the data, its source, and its nature. The quality of the questions is highly important, as it impacts the quality of the data and subsequently, the insights derived.

◆ Questions in data analytics can be descriptive, inferential, predictive, or prescriptive, each requiring different types and levels of analysis.

◆ Data collection is a systematic process of gathering and measuring information on variables of interest, involving meticulous planning to ensure accuracy and reliability of the collected data, which can be either quantitative (numerical) or qualitative (non-numerical).

◆ Depending on the research goals, different techniques such as surveys, interviews, observations, or the use of pre-existing information may be employed for data collection.

◆ Data cleansing is an essential phase in data analytics where potential data inconsistencies or flaws are identified and fixed to improve data quality.

◆ The detailed processes of data cleansing include data validation, data screening, diagnosing phase, de-duplication, handling of invalid data, dealing with missing data, and dealing with outliers.

◆ The data analysis process comprises four key functional elements: descriptive, diagnostic/inferential, predictive, and prescriptive analytics.

◆ It's vital to select the right data analytics techniques based on the nature of the data and research objectives, which could range from regression analysis to machine learning algorithms and advanced analytics.

◆ Data visualization is a critical part of the data analytics process, converting raw data into graphic formats to make it easier to understand and analyze. The type of visualization to use depends on the message that needs to be communicated.

◆ After visualization, data needs to be effectively shared, keeping in mind the level of data analytics knowledge of the intended audience.

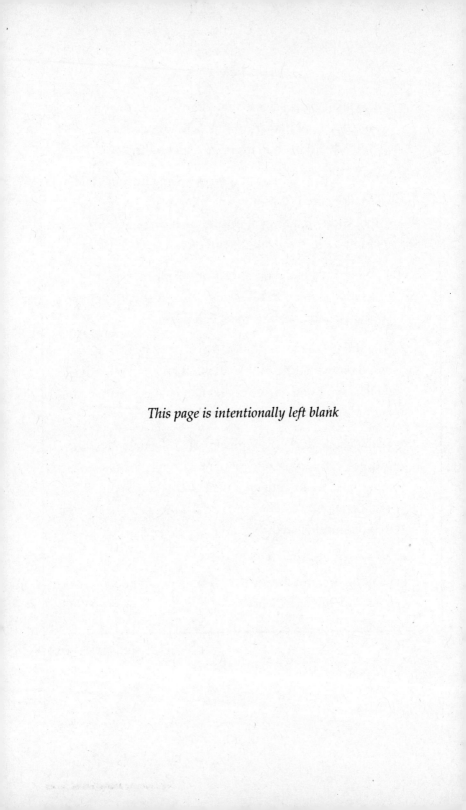

This page is intentionally left blank

Chapter 6

Big Data Analytics

Big data analytics finds use across various industries, promoting growth, efficiency, and innovation. It involves examining, analyzing, and interpreting large and diverse sets of data, known as 'big data', to discover patterns, correlations, trends, and insights that can guide decision-making within organizations.

The key learning objectives of this chapter include the reader's understanding of the following:

- More details regarding what big data is
- The challenges of big data analytics
- The technologies of big data analytics
- Several case studies of big data analytics
- The future of big data analytics

6.1 What is Big Data?

We have seen a significant trend toward the "datafication" of social and environmental activities in this digital age[150]. Every interaction and every activity generates a data trail. We collectively refer to this enormous digital footprint as "big data." But what exactly is big data?

Big data is a term used to describe data sets whose size or kind are too complex for traditional relational databases to properly store, manage, and process. It consists of numerous types of data in amounts ranging from terabytes to zettabytes, including structured, semi-structured, and unstructured data from various sources. In other words, big data refers to the high volume, high velocity (the rate at which data is captured and the rate of data flow), and high variety of data[151].

The different types of data structures are: unstructured, quasi-structured, semi-structured, and structured. It has been estimated that 80 to 90% of future data growth comes from the non-structured data.

Artificial intelligence (AI), mobile technology, social media, and the Internet of Things (IoT) are commonplace in the digital age, which contributes to data complexity and introduces new types and sources of data. These developments in technology have produced a dynamic environment where data is continuously produced in real-time and at a never-before-seen scale.

---

150. Plato. Stanford.Edu. 2020. Scientific Research and Big Data. Stanford Encyclopedia of Philosophy. URL: https://plato.stanford.edu/entries/science-big-data/ .

151. Banik, A., Bandyopadhyay, S.K. 2016. Big Data-A Review on Analysing 3Vs. Journal of Scientific and Engineering Research, 2016, 3(1). ISSN: 2394-2630.

While the term "big data" may be contemporary, the phenomenon itself is not. Many contend that techniques like those used in the management and analysis of big data have been around for a long time and go by many names, including statistics, analytics, and business intelligence.

Big data is used and influenced widely throughout various fields and industries. Big data is employed in the field of healthcare to analyze numerous patient data types, such as genomic sequences, physiological measures, and individual responses to treatment, ultimately leading to better diagnosis and care[152]. Another example is how transportation data on traffic flow, geographic and environmental variables, and human behavior are combined to create safety measures for driverless cars.

Academic institutions and libraries, which are frequently viewed as pillars of knowledge, are also included. Librarians are faced with the difficulty of figuring out their role in the processing of big data and how to use it to build better services due to the enormous and complex data collected in these institutions[153]. In fact, today there is much more available data than our ability to do something with it.

---

152. Asri, H, 2015. Big Data in healthcare: Challenges and Opportunities. Big Data in healthcare: Challenges and Opportunities, 1, 1-5.

153. Garoufallou, E., Gaitanou, P. 2021. Big Data: Opportunities and Challenges in Libraries, a Systematic Literature Review. Association of College & Research Libraries, Vol.82, No.3 (2021). URL: https://crl.acrl.org/index.php/crl/article/view/24918/32769 .

| Figure 6.1 | Illustrates the great amount of data generated in the last few years. |

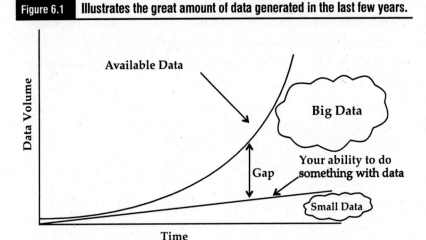

Source: Stewart, M. 2019. Handling Big Datasets for Machine Learning. Towards Data Science. URL: https://towardsdatascience.com/machine-learning-with-big-data-86bcb39f2f0b.

 Fun Fact

Did you know that currently, Google processes more than 40,000 search requests per second on average? That amounts to more than 3.5 billion searches daily and 1.2 trillion searches annually globally[154]. Big data analytics has its playground in this enormous amount of data.

Text analytics, machine learning, predictive analytics, data mining, statistics, and natural language processing are some of the methods used in big data analysis. With the help of these state-of-the-art analytics methods, analysts, researchers, and business users may now quickly and more accurately make decisions by utilizing data that was previously unavailable or unsuitable.

---

154. Internet Live Stats. 2023. Google Search Statistics. Internet Live Stats. Retrieved in November 2023 from https://www.internetlivestats.com/google-search-statistics/.

To sum it up, big data has already begun to transform the way we live, work, and think. The ongoing development of big data technology offers both benefits and difficulties. It is crucial that we create efficient strategies to use this data to the advantage of society, business, academia, and government as we continue to produce and collect more data[155].

6.2 Challenges of Big Data Analytics

Big data analytics (BDA) has demonstrated a remarkable capacity for delivering insights that support reasoned decision-making[156]. But despite its size and strength, big data poses a special set of problems that companies and data scientists must address.

High data volume, velocity, and variety

Big data refers to huge, diverse, and rapidly growing databases and is characterized by the "3Vs" - volume, velocity, and variety[157]. The vast amount of data presents a formidable challenge because it necessitates extensive storage capacities. Additionally, the high rate of data generation necessitates real-time or nearly real-time processing, which puts traditional systems' processing power to the test. The variety of data, including structured, unstructured,

155. Obradovic, Z. 2023. Big Data. LiebertPub. Volume 11, No.3, June 2023. ISSN: 2167-6461.

156. Sivarajah, U., Kamal, M.M., Irani, Z., Weerakkody, V. 2017. Critical analysis of Big Data challenges and analytical methods. Journal of Business Research, Volume 70, January 2017, Pages 263-286.

157. Xu, Z., Shi, Y. 2016. Exploring Big Data Analysis: Fundamental Scientific Problems. Ann. Data. Sci. 2, 363–372 (2015). https://doi.org/10.1007/s40745-015-0063-7 .

and semi-structured data, necessitates the use of powerful and adaptable data management and processing tools[158].

Bottlenecks in scalability and storage

Organizations frequently struggle to scale their storage and processing capacities in response to the constant rise in data volume and velocity. Scalability is a problem for data-intensive applications since they need adequate storage and processing mechanisms to accommodate enormous volumes of data[159]. Massive data storage also frequently causes bottlenecks in the data analysis pipeline, which slows down the entire procedure.

Noise accumulation and spurious correlation

Big data often results in the accumulation of noise, which is irrelevant or incorrect data that might skew results, due to its increased volume and dimensionality. This buildup of noise can lead to erroneous correlations, which show associations between variables that don't exist. Such erroneous associations may result in misleading conclusions and poor decision-making.

Incidental endogeneity and measurement errors

In big data, endogeneity problems, where predictors in a model are linked with the error term, frequently occur and impair the accuracy of the findings. Statistical inferences may be incorrect because of this incidental endogeneity.[160] Furthermore, because big data comes from so many different sources, measurement

158. Rawat, R., Yadav, R. 2021. Big Data: Big Data Analysis, Issues and Challenges and Technologies. v 2021 IOP Conf. Ser.: Mater. Sci. Eng. 1022 012014.

159. Fan, J., Han, F., Liu, H. 2014. Challenges of Big Data Analysis. National Science Review, 1:293-324, 2014, https://doi.org/10.1093/nsr/nwt032 .

160. Asri, H, 2015. Big Data in healthcare: Challenges and Opportunities. Big Data in healthcare: Challenges and Opportunities, 1, 1-5.

errors are frequent and have a substantial impact on the accuracy of the data and subsequent analyses.

Complex data visualization and analysis

Big data involves more than just managing huge amounts of data; it also involves interpreting that data. Big data analysis, which includes data collection, storage, management, analytics, and visualization, poses several difficulties. To extract valuable insights from the data, these stages' complexity frequently necessitates the employment of sophisticated analytics and visualization tools.[161]

Requirement for robust infrastructure

Big data processing demands a stable and trustworthy infrastructure. The computational demands of big data are frequently not met by traditional systems. To effectively handle and analyze huge datasets, high-performance computing systems and parallel processing techniques are therefore required[162].

In conclusion, big data analytics has enormous potential but also poses formidable obstacles. To successfully manage and gain insights from big data, organizations wanting to use it must be aware of these obstacles and invest in the right tools, technologies, and procedures. In addition to giving firms a competitive advantage, overcoming these obstacles will promote innovation and growth over the long term.

---

161. Banik, A., Bandyopadhyay, S.K. 2016. Big Data-A Review on Analysing 3Vs. Journal of Scientific and Engineering Research, 2016, 3(1). ISSN: 2394-2630.

162. Heiss, A. 2019. Big Data Challenges in Big Science. Computing and Software for Big Science 3, 15 (2019). https://doi.org/10.1007/s41781-019-0030-7 .

6.3 Technologies for Big Data Analytics

The practice of big data analytics (BDA) has become crucial in the current digital environment. BDA uses numerous important technologies to deliver substantial insights for various disciplines, from healthcare to business to smart sustainable cities[163]. It is characterized by the analysis of huge amounts of varied data from multiple sources at unprecedented speeds[164].

Cloud computing is one of the fundamental technologies that underpin BDA. The cloud allows scalable, economical solutions for managing big data volumes by acting as a platform for data storage and computation. It enables companies of all sizes to access the power of big data without needing to make substantial infrastructure investments[165].

For instance, big data analytics-as-a-service (BDaaS) utilizes the cloud's scalability to eliminate the communication gap between data scientists and security experts. These experts can avoid the skills gap in both the security and data science domains by using BDaaS to jointly deploy analytics processes in real-time[166].

---

163. Corsi, A., de Souza, F.F., Pagani, R.N. et al. 2021. Big data analytics as a tool for fighting pandemics: a systematic review of literature. Journal of Ambient Intelligence and Humanized Computing 12, 9163–9180 (2021). https://doi.org/10.1007/s12652-020-02617-4 .

164. Bibri, S.E., Krogstie, J. 2017. The core enabling technologies of big data analytics and context-aware computing for smart sustainable cities: a review and synthesis. Journal of Big Data 4, 38 (2017).

165. Balachandran, B.M., Prasad, S. 2017. Challenges and Benefits of Deploying Big Data Analytics in the Cloud for Business Intelligence. Procedia Computer Science, Volume 112, 2017, Pages 1112-1122.

166. Ardagna, C.A., Bellandi, V., Damiani, E., Bezzi, M., Hebert, C. 2021. Big Data Analytics-as-a-Service: Bridging the gap between security experts and data scientists. Computers & Electrical Engineering, Volume 93, July 2021, 107215.

Data generation for BDA is also greatly aided by the Internet of Things (IoT). The growth of big data is fueled by IoT devices like sensors and smartphones that continuously collect and transmit data. Data from IoT devices, for instance, can enhance global health initiatives, patient care, and diagnostics in the healthcare industry[167].

In terms of analysis, large data can be effectively analyzed using two main technologies: machine learning (ML) and artificial intelligence (AI). While AI can simulate human-like decision-making processes, ML algorithms can learn from the data to make predictions and suggestions, increasing efficiency and accuracy in difficult jobs[168].

For instance, deep learning-based algorithms have proven their ability to anticipate complicated weather patterns from huge data sets in the field of weather forecasting[169]. Similar to this, AI techniques have been applied to healthcare to optimize patient care and provide decision support.

Another technology for big data analytics is MapReduce. MapReduce and similar frameworks are essential for processing and analyzing massive data in parallel across distributed clusters. The Map function processes and organizes data into key-value

167. Khanra, S., Dhir, A., Islam, A.K.M.N., Mantymaki, M. 2020. Big data analytics in healthcare: a systematic literature review. Journal of Enterprise Information System, Volume 14, 2020 - Issue 7, https://doi.org/10.1080/17517575.2020.1812005 .

168. Ojokoh, B.A., Samuel, O.W., Omisore, O.M., Sarumi, O.A., Idowu, P.A., Chimusa, E.R., Darwish, A., Adekoya, A.F., Katsriku, F. 2020. Big data, analytics and artificial intelligence for sustainability. Scientific African, Volume 9, September 2020, e00551, https://doi.org/10.1016/j.sciaf.2020.e00551 .

169. Ren, X., Li, X., Ren, K., Song, J., Xu, Z., Deng, K., Wang, X. 2021. Deep Learning-Based Weather Prediction: A Survey. Elsevier Journal of Big Data Research, Volume 23, 15 February 2021, 100178, https://doi.org/10.1016/j.bdr.2020.100178 .

pairs, which are then processed by the reduce function to produce insightful results[170].

Quick Tips

Optimizing your "Map" and "Reduce" functions for efficiency is crucial when utilizing MapReduce in big data analytics[171]. Write clear, simple code that efficiently filters and arranges your data during the "Map" phase. For the "Reduce" step to manage the aggregation smoothly, make sure it is as lean as feasible. In this manner, you may process enormous datasets more quickly and effectively with MapReduce tasks, saving time and computational resources.

Although these technologies offer strong resources for handling and interpreting big data, it's important to be aware that they can present difficulties. In a time of growing datafication, privacy and security are top priorities[172]. Big data's analytical power also necessitates ethical considerations surrounding its application and potential for abuse. Despite these obstacles, big data analytics holds the potential to inform decision-making and resolve complicated issues.

170. Balachandran, B.M., Prasad, S. 2017. Challenges and Benefits of Deploying Big Data Analytics in the Cloud for Business Intelligence. Procedia Computer Science, Volume 112, 2017, Pages 1112-1122.

171. Thanekar, S.A., Subrahmanyam, K., Bagwan, A.B. 2016. Big Data and MapReduce Challenges, Opportunities and Trends. International Journal of Electrical and Computer Engineering (IJECE), Vol. 6, No. 6, December 2016, pp. 2911~2919, ISSN: 2088-8708, DOI: 10.11591/ijece.v6i6.10555.

172. Ardagna, C.A., Bellandi, V., Damiani, E., Bezzi, M., Hebert, C. 2021. Big Data Analytics-as-a-Service: Bridging the gap between security experts and data scientists. Computers & Electrical Engineering, Volume 93, July 2021, 107215.

6.4 Case Studies in Big Data Analytics

Companies are operating in a completely new way thanks to big data, which gives them a competitive edge by enabling them to comprehend and strategically exploit complicated client behaviors[173]. This subchapter's case studies on big data analytics will demonstrate how various industries use this tool to gain competitive advantages.

Case Study 1: Walmart and retail analytics

Walmart, one of the biggest retailers in the world, leverages big data to improve the shopping experience for its customers. Walmart uses data mining to find trends in consumer behavior that they can then utilize to provide tailored product suggestions. Big data analytics were used by Walmart to improve consumer conversion rates, securing its position as a top international retailer[174].

Case Study 2: Netflix entertainment analytics

Netflix uses big data in the entertainment industry to analyze viewing behavior and adjust content accordingly. Around 75% of viewer behavior is influenced by personalized recommendations that are generated using data from viewer activity. This strategy

---

173. Baesens, B. 2014. Analytics in a Big Data World: The Essential Guide to Data Science and its Applications. Wiley Online Library. ISBN:9781118892701, Online ISBN:9781119204183, DOI: 10.1002/9781119204183.

174. Singh, M., Lilo Jnr, R., Ghutla, B., Aessaan. 2017. M. Walmart's Sales Data Analysis - A Big Data Analytics Perspective. In Proceedings of The Conference: 2017 4th Asia-Pacific World Congress on Computer Science and Engineering (APWC on CSE). DOI:10.1109/APWConCSE.2017.00028.

not only enhances the viewing experience but also greatly aids in business expansion[175].

Netflix's recommendation engine is a sophisticated technology that customizes content recommendations for every user. To determine preferences, it makes use of a variety of data points, such as watch history, user ratings, and search queries. In order to suggest related content, the system also takes into account the nature of the shows, such as their genre and performers. Viewing patterns on various platforms (phones, tablets, and TVs) are taken into consideration, along with the context of program pauses and re-watches. Furthermore, the amount of time a user spends on end credits—also referred to as credit calculation—helps determine interest levels. With this all-encompassing strategy, Netflix can offer every user a unique and captivating viewing experience.

Case Study 3: Aetna's health analytics

Big data is used by healthcare giant Aetna to enhance patient outcomes. The business can concentrate on treating one or two risk factors that will have the biggest effects on enhancing health by reviewing the outcomes of tests that detect metabolic syndrome and evaluating risk factors. According to Petersen (2023), a significant number of patients benefit from this focused strategy, which improves medication compliance and promotes proactive health checks.

Case Study 4: American Express and predictive analytics

American Express created algorithms that examine previous transactions and other factors to predict potential churn in order to employ big data analytics to predict client loyalty.

---

175. Van Es, K. 2022. Netflix & Big Data: The Strategic Ambivalence of an Entertainment Company. Sage Pub Journals, Journal of Television & New Media, DOI: 10.1177/15274764221125745.

To forecast possible client loss, the business used complex algorithms to evaluate enormous volumes of transaction data in addition to other pertinent customer data. AmEx wants to be proactive in retaining its clients by spotting early indicators of dissatisfaction or diminished engagement.

American Express's churn prediction model makes use of a number of data sources, such as transaction history, customer service exchanges, and engagement levels across AmEx platforms. The process of developing new variables, or features, that capture the underlying patterns of consumer behavior that can point to a risk of churn is known as feature engineering, and it is essential to predictive modeling. Metrics including shifts in transaction volume, transaction frequency, purchase kinds, and customer service interactions are examples of features. To anticipate the loss of clients, American Express uses machine learning algorithms.

According to reports[176], American Express can detect up to 24% of U.S. accounts that would shut during the following four months by using this data-driven method. Early detection makes targeted interventions possible, which can raise customer satisfaction and retention rates and eventually boost the bottom line and customer loyalty of the business.

---

176. Ajah, I.A., Nweke, H.F. 2019. Big Data and Business Analytics: Trends, Platforms, Success Factors and Applications. Big Data Cogn. Comput. 2019, 3(2), 32; https://doi.org/10.3390/bdcc3020032.

By examining historical transaction data to anticipate spending patterns and identify possible fraud, American Express uses predictive analytics to enhance customer experience and stop fraud[177]. Atypical high-value transactions are flagged in real-time, allowing the business to promptly stop fraud. By lowering fraudulent activity, this tactic protects consumers and helps American Express save millions of dollars annually.

Case Study 5: Google Analytics for search and advertising

Finally, the internet giant Google uses big data to improve its fundamental search and ad-serving algorithms. It continuously creates new services and products using big data analytics[178]. The company's effective big data strategy is essential to preserving its position as the top search engine in the world.

To process and analyze petabytes of data, Google has developed and released open-source tools like Bigtable, TensorFlow, and MapReduce. The volume of data that Google gathers from user interactions, web searches, and other sources is compatible with these technologies.

Google utilizes artificial intelligence and machine learning in conjunction with big data to enhance its search engines[179], comprehend user intent, and forecast which advertisements will be most pertinent to consumers. To analyze search queries,

177. Banarescu, A. 2015. Detecting and Preventing Fraud with Data Analytics. Procedia Economics and Finance 32 (2015) 1827 – 1836. DOI: 10.1016/S2212-5671(15)01485-9.

178. Dulal, R. 2016. Big Data and Google File System. Proceedings of the Conference: 8th National Students' Conference on Information TechnologyAt: Kathmandu, Nepal.

179. Gorman, W. 2018. Machine Learning & Big Data at Google. Google Cloud, ML Workshop.

content, and user behavior, methods like natural language processing (NLP), deep learning, and reinforcement learning are essential.

The key to Google's success as the most popular search engine in the world is its adept application of big data analytics. Google maintains its market leadership and drives revenue growth by consistently enhancing the relevance and accuracy of search results and ad targeting, while also improving user experience and advertising platform performance.

In summary, big data analytics is being used across industries to leverage the power of data, whether it be in retail, entertainment, finance, healthcare, or technology. It helps in deciphering complex patterns, foreseeing trends, improving customer satisfaction, and boosting corporate results. These case studies demonstrate the revolutionary potential of big data analytics and give an idea of what data-driven decision-making may look like in the future. Big data enthusiasts will undoubtedly have a competitive advantage in today's economy.

6.5 The Future of Big Data Analytics

The world's transformation into a "datafied" society has left a massive digital imprint, and the resulting big data has emerged as a research gold mine. Big data analytics will be shaped by a variety of new technology developments, inventive approaches, and emerging challenges.

Future developments in data analytics will heavily rely on artificial intelligence (AI) and machine learning (ML). These sophisticated ML algorithms can quickly process and evaluate enormous amounts of data while enhancing their performance. Together with predictive and prescriptive analytics, this constant self-improvement equips organizations with insightful data.

Additionally, the idea of "augmented analytics," which refers to the automation of insights using machine learning and natural language processing (NLP), is gaining popularity. By offering a method to handle the difficulties of expanding data volumes, it represents a promising advancement in big data analytics[180].

Big data analytics in the healthcare industry offers better patient outcomes through individualized treatment plans[181]. Studies on population nutrition and traffic safety are two more applications of big data analytics that have promise.

Another industry where big data analytics and AI have made significant strides is education. Educational institutions can provide tailored learning experiences and better evaluation techniques by utilizing these technologies[182].

Despite the enormous advantages of big data analytics, it's critical to comprehend their difficulties. To maximize value, businesses must consider the many kinds of analytics applications

---

180. Minu, M.S., Ahmad, Z. 2020. Augmented Analytics: The Future of Business Intelligence. ManTech Publications, Recent Trends in Computer Science and Software Technology Volume 5 Issue 1, DOI: http://doi.org/10.5281/zenodo.3757837.

181. Cozzoli N, Salvatore FP, Faccilongo N, Milone M. 2022. How can big data analytics be used for healthcare organization management? Literary framework and future research from a systematic review. BMC Health Serv Res. 2022 Jun 22;22(1):809. doi: 10.1186/s12913-022-08167-z. PMID: 35733192; PMCID: PMC9213639.

182. Luan, H., Geczy, P., Lai, H., Gobert, J., Yang, S.J.H., Ogata, H/, Baltes, J., Guerra, R., Li, P., Tsai, C.C. 2020. Challenges and Future Directions of Big Data and Artificial Intelligence in Education. Front Psychol. 2020 Oct 19;11:580820. doi: 10.3389/fpsyg.2020.580820. PMID: 33192896; PMCID: PMC7604529.

and tools[183].

Data management and storage are also made more difficult by the exponential development of data. Additionally, there is a growing gap in the availability of skilled data scientists and analysts, necessitating the development of novel solutions.

Businesses are anticipated to completely operationalize their big data plans as time goes on, which will increase the amount of streaming data and analytics infrastructures. The use of big data analytics will continue to grow and become integral to strategic company planning. To get to this future, rigorous preparation and strategic investments are needed to successfully traverse the changing big data analytics world.

In conclusion, big data analytics has a bright future ahead of it, one that is rife with both potential and difficulties. Businesses must make sure they have the skills and resources to take advantage of the opportunities.

---

183. Sivarajah, U., Kamal, M.M., Irani, Z., Weerakkody, V. 2017. Critical analysis of Big Data challenges and analytical methods. Journal of Business Research, Volume 70, January 2017, Pages 263-286.

Quiz

1. **What is "big data"?**

   a. Small chunks of structured data

   b. Data sets that are too complex for traditional databases to properly store, manage, and process

   c. Only structured data from a single source

   d. Random data collected from the Internet

2. **What are the types of data included in big data?**

   a. Structured data only

   b. Unstructured data only

   c. Semi-structured data only

   d. Structured, semi-structured, and unstructured data

3. **Which of the following fields is not influenced by big data?**

   a. Healthcare

   b. Transportation

   c. Academic institutions and libraries

   d. None of the above

4. **Which of the following is a potential risk of big data?**

   a. It can help uncover insights.

   b. Data can be misused and misinterpreted when it falls into the wrong hands.

   c. It can be used to resolve problems.

   d. It can improve the world.

5. **What are the "3Vs" that characterize big data?**

   a. Volume, variation, variety

   b. Volume, velocity, variety

   c. Velocity, volume, versatility

   d. Variety, volume, visibility

6. **Which of the following is a major issue associated with data-intensive applications in big data analytics?**

   a. Lack of data sources

   b. Scalability

   c. Irrelevant data sources

   d. Easy data visualization

7. **What does noise accumulation in big data refer to?**

   a. Increased data storage

   b. Rapid growth of databases

   c. Irrelevant or incorrect data that might skew results

   d. Errors in data visualization tools

8. In the context of big data, what is incidental endogeneity?

   a. A situation where predictors in a model are linked with the error term

   b. The occurrence of spurious correlations due to noise accumulation

   c. The process of scaling storage and processing capacities

   d. The complexity involved in big data visualization and analysis

9. Which of the following fields can benefit from big data analytics (BDA)?

   a. Healthcare

   b. Business

   c. Smart sustainable cities

   d. All of the above

10. What does big data analytics-as-a-service (BDaaS) utilize to eliminate the communication gap between data scientists and security experts?

   a. Machine learning

   b. Cloud's scalability

   c. Internet of Things

   d. MapReduce

Answers	1 – b	2 – d	3 – d	4 – b	5 – b
	6 – b	7 – c	8 – a	9 – d	10 – b

Chapter Summary

◆ The term "big data" is one of the key concepts in this field of data analytics.

◆ Big data is the term used to describe massive, intricate datasets gathered from various sources that are too large or complex for typical databases to handle.

◆ Data complexity has increased due to the digital age and technological breakthroughs like artificial intelligence (AI), mobile technology, social media, and the Internet of Things, which have led to the continuous real-time production of this data at previously unheard-of scales.

◆ Big data analytics, despite its potential for valuable insights, presents unique challenges: the 3 Vs (high volume, velocity, variety), bottlenecks in scalability and storage, noise accumulation and spurious correlation, incidental endogeneity and measurement errors, complex data visualization and analysis, requirement for robust infrastructure.

◆ To analyze vast and diverse data, big data analytics (BDA) makes use of critical technologies like cloud computing, the Internet of Things (IoT), machine learning (ML), and artificial intelligence (AI).

◆ These technologies provide important insights across a range of industries, including healthcare, business, and smart sustainable cities.

- ◆ Several case studies on big data analytics were presented in this chapter to demonstrate how various industries use big data analytics to gain competitive advantages: Walmart and retail analytics, Netflix entertainment analytics, American Express and predictive analytics, Aetna's health analytics, and Google analytics for search and advertising.

- ◆ Future advances in data analytics will heavily rely on machine learning (ML) and artificial intelligence (AI), enabling quick processing and evaluation of enormous data quantities.

- ◆ The volume of streaming data and analytics infrastructures will increase as businesses are expected to fully operationalize their big data strategies. Consequently, for organizations to succeed in the evolving big data analytics landscape, careful planning and strategic investments are required.

Chapter 7

Ethics and Privacy in Data Analytics

A s data analytics continues to evolve, striking a balance between innovation and ethical responsibility becomes increasingly challenging but imperative. Businesses, researchers, and policymakers alike must commit to responsible data practices to ensure a fair and transparent digital future.

The key learning objectives of this chapter include the reader's understanding of the following:

- The human factor, privacy and consent, and discrimination and fairness in data analytics

- The description of the three significant privacy concerns: improper data collection methods, insufficient data security, and the unethical use of data

- A description of the two main types of regulations: data privacy laws and financial regulations;

- The best practices that must be adopted by companies to ensure they comply with the regulations
- The likely future of ethics and privacy in data analytics.

7.1 Ethics in Data Analytics

The oversimplified perspective that portrays data analytics as a neutral, all-knowing process may hide some crucial ethical problems. Let's talk about these points to comprehend the ethical context of data analytics.

7.1.1 The human factor

The human factor in the analysis process is one of the key ethical debates in data analytics. Data science is frequently misunderstood to be an analysis process that uses only automated techniques. This viewpoint could overshadow the importance of the process's human decision-makers[184]. Data scientists' involvement and strategic guidance are required for data analytics tools.

However, because they decide which data to take into account and how to interpret them, these professionals' decisions might occasionally result in biases. To ensure that data analytics is a transparent process, giving proper credit to the human effort, and recognizing the possibility of human biases, ethical consideration must be given.

184. Markham, A. N., Tiidenberg, K., & Herman, A. 2018. Ethics as Methods: Doing Ethics in the Era of Big Data Research—Introduction. Social Media + Society, 4(3). https://doi.org/10.1177/2056305118784502 .

7.1.2 Privacy and consent

In the case of Cambridge Analytica, millions of users' personal information was unlawfully obtained and exploited for political advertising. Significant privacy concerns were brought to light by this controversy, and it also raised ethical concerns about the use of data to sway elections and voter behavior. The Cambridge Analytica incident serves as a reminder of the dangers of exploiting personal data without explicit authorization in light of the increasing relevance of data privacy[185].

To guarantee that data is handled responsibly and ethically, ethical standards must be upheld as dealing with sensitive personal data is a common part of data analytics. Important ethical considerations in this regard include appropriate anonymization procedures, secure data storage, and the use of personal data only with informed consent.

7.1.3 Discrimination and fairness

Another important topic in data analytics ethics is algorithmic discrimination. Algorithms may unintentionally reinforce or even exacerbate societal prejudices that already exist in the data they are trained on as they learn from it[186].

For instance, if historical data shows that specific racial or socioeconomic groups have a record of loan defaults, an algorithm

---

185. Baumer, B., Garcia, R.L., Kim, A.Y., Kinnaird, K.M., Ott, M.Q. 2022. Integrating Data Science Ethics Into an Undergraduate Major: A Case Study. Taylor & Francis Group, Journal of Statistics and Data Science Education, Volume 30, 2022, Issue 1, DOI: https://doi.org/10.1080/26939169.2022.2038041 .

186. Saltz, J., Dewar, N. 2019. Data science ethical considerations: a systematic literature review and proposed project framework. Springer Link, Journal of Ethics and Information Technology, 21, pages 197–208 (2019), DOI: https://doi.org/10.1007/s10676-019-09502-5 .

might link increased credit risk with these groups. This poses a serious ethical problem since it could result in biased outcomes that marginalize some groups.

It's crucial to create algorithms with fairness in mind, continuously check their output for indications of bias, and recalibrate them as necessary to encourage fair and equal results to mitigate this.

In conclusion, a wide range of complicated topics, including human involvement, privacy and consent, and fairness are covered in the debate on the ethics of data analytics. These ethical issues will grow more significant as data science develops, influencing how we manage and interpret data in a world that depends on it more and more.

With this knowledge, we may better recognize the significance of ethical considerations in data analytics and work to create a society where data is used responsibly.

 Did you know that over 2.5 quintillion bytes of data are created every day[187], yet much of this data contains personal information? GDPR and other ethical guidelines, as well as privacy laws, are intended to safeguard sensitive data in the data analytics industry. Notwithstanding these steps, a survey reveals a substantial ethical oversight gap: just 52% of businesses verify that their analytics solutions adhere to ethics standards.

---

187. Namjoshi, J., Rawat, M. 2022. Role of smart manufacturing in industry 4.0. Materials Today, Volume 63, 2022, Pages 475-478. DOI: https://doi.org/10.1016/j.matpr.2022.03.620.

7.2 Privacy in Data Analytics

Data analytics can be quite a boon, providing unparalleled insights into customer behavior, predictive modeling, and operational efficiency. But like all great powers, it comes with great responsibility, particularly concerning privacy. So, let's break it down, shall we?

First off, the advantages of data analytics in, say, marketing are undeniable. By understanding customer behavior, companies can enhance their marketing strategies. However, this does beg the question: How much should companies know about you? Researchers have found that trust in business practices is crucial to responsibly handling this data[188].

There are three significant privacy concerns you should be aware of. These include improper data collection methods, insufficient data security, and the unethical use of data. Fortunately, there are ways for businesses to mitigate these risks.

7.2.1 Improper data collection

A lot of companies collect more data than they actually need. This is a ticking time bomb when it comes to privacy concerns. As a step of the data analytics process, data collection offers unique opportunities for implementing privacy measures early in the process, which can ensure "privacy by design"[189]. According to the

188. Petrescu, M., Krishen, A.S. 2018. Analyzing the analytics: data privacy concerns. Springer Link, Journal of Marketing Analytics 6, 41–43 (2018). https://doi.org/10.1057/s41270-018-0034-x .

189. General Data Protection Regulation (GDPR). Art. 25 GDPR. Data protection by design and by default. General Data Protection Regulation of the European Union, Article 25. URL: https://gdpr-info.eu/art-25-gdpr/ .

General Data Protection Regulation (GDPR), data collection is the responsibility of the processor.

7.2.2 Insufficient data security

If the data isn't encrypted and properly safeguarded, the risks of a data breach increase. Such incidents can have catastrophic effects, both for the company and the individuals whose data is compromised[190].

7.2.3 Unethical use of data

Using data for purposes other than what was initially agreed upon is not just bad manners; it's an invasion of privacy. Individuals must trust that organizations will meet their commitments, act reliably, and not use their data in an unethical or opportunistic way[191].

 Quick Tips

By creating and rigorously enforcing a data ethics policy in line with moral and legal requirements, businesses may stop unethical data practices. Employee data handling training, getting active consent for data gathering, guaranteeing openness in data usage, and upholding stringent data access rules should all be important components of this strategy. Conducting routine audits is vital to guarantee continued adherence to these moral guidelines.

---

190. Maillart, T. 2015. The Extreme Risk of Personal Data Breaches & The Erosion of Privacy. The European Physical Journal B 89(1). DOI:10.1140/epjb/e2015-60754-4 .

191. Someh, I., Davern, M., Breidbach, C. F., & Shanks, G. (2019). Ethical Issues in Big Data Analytics: A Stakeholder Perspective. Communications of the Association for Information Systems, 44. https://doi.org/10.17705/1CAIS.04434

7.2.4 Predictive analytics and privacy

Predictive analytics brings up a particular privacy concern. By utilizing the data left by millions of other users, predictive analytics predicts sensitive information about individuals or groups from less sensitive or more easily accessible information (proxy data), possibly without the knowledge of the data subjects (Figure 7.1). This poses a new problem for data ethics and privacy regulation as, in this case, privacy is jeopardized by information that is revealed by several people rather than by the subjects themselves (i.e., by networked service users as uninvited providers of training data). If the information shared by numerous unconnected, possibly even anonymous users aids in estimating sensitive information about users who might not be represented in the training data, it presents a qualitatively new data protection risk[192].

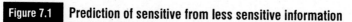

Figure 7.1 **Prediction of sensitive from less sensitive information**

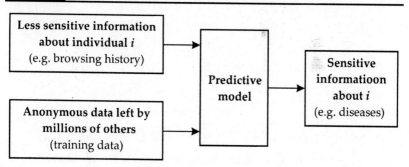

Source: Long, C. et al. 2015. Data Science & Big Data Analytics: Discovering, Analyzing, Visualizing and Presenting Data. John Wiley & Sons, Inc., Canada. ISBN: 978-1-118-87613-8.

192. Muehlhoff, R. 2021. Predictive privacy: towards an applied ethics of data analytics. Ethics and Information Technology. DOI: https://doi.org/10.1007/s10676-021-09606-x.

The rules of data privacy are changing, largely because people are becoming more aware of the value of their personal data. This recognition has given rise to new kinds of data custodians and representatives, who facilitate data-sharing arrangements based on consent.

Some argue that data analytics challenges fundamental privacy protections, while others believe that our privacy requirements are obstacles to the benefits of advanced analytics. But, in reality, big data and privacy are not mutually exclusive. It's more about striking a balance between the two[193].

Data analytics offers extraordinary benefits, but it's not a free-for-all. The companies that will succeed in this landscape are those that respect privacy as a fundamental human right. They'll collect only the data they need, keep it safe, and use it responsibly. Most importantly, these companies will build a bridge of trust with you, the consumer, making it a win-win for everyone involved.

So, as we delve deeper into this era of digital transformation, let's not lose sight of the importance of respecting each other's privacy. The exciting advancements in data analytics should empower us all, not compromise our fundamental rights.

7.3 Regulatory Frameworks for Data Analytics

It's essential to understand why regulation is crucial in data analytics. As data becomes increasingly valuable, the potential for misuse grows exponentially. Here, regulations work like traffic

---

193. Mehmood, A., Natgunanathan, I., Xiang, Y., Hua, G., Song, G. 2016. Protection of Big Data Privacy. IEEE Access, 2169-3536, Volume 4, Digital Object Identifier 10.1109/ ACCESS.2016.2558446.

lights, guiding your journey through data analytics while keeping you and others safe.

There are 2 main types of regulations: data privacy laws and financial regulations.

GDPR in Europe, CCPA in the U.S., and the Chinese Personal Data Protection Law (PIPL) are game changers in data privacy systems of laws. These privacy laws control the processing of personal data by imposing requirements on businesses and giving users rights, which may have an influence on value for both businesses (by increasing costs) and users (by boosting utility from greater privacy).

Fun Fact

People now have the "right to be forgotten," which enables them to ask for the deletion of their personal data, thanks to the GDPR[194]. Google consequently received more than 2.4 million requests to use this privilege to remove URLs from its search engine. Companies now need to make sure they can efficiently forget data in addition to being able to analyze it with expertise. This has completely changed the landscape of data analytics!

Regardless of the business models used, entities handling substantial amounts of personal data are required to adhere to relevant data protection laws. In Europe, four key components, according to the European Data Protection Supervisor (EDPS), are

---

194. Razmetaeva, Y. 2020. The Right to Be Forgotten in the European Perspective. TalTech Journal of European Studies 10(1): 58-76. DOI:10.1515/bjes-2020-0004.

necessary for the responsible and sustainable development of big data[195]:

- Organizations need to be much more transparent about how they process personal data

- Users need to have more control over how their data is used

- User-friendly data protection needs to be incorporated into their products and services

- Organizations need to take greater responsibility for their actions

These components are depicted as well in Figure 7.2.

Figure 7.2 **The four components necessary for the responsible and sustainable development of big data**

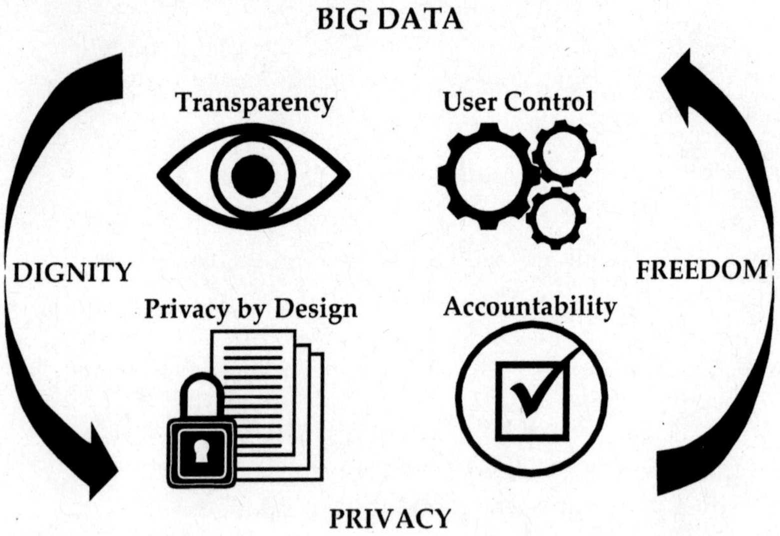

Source: European Data Protection Supervisor. 2015. Meeting the challenges of big data. EDPS Publication, Opinion 7/2015.

---

195. European Data Protection Supervisor. 2015. Meeting the challenges of big data. EDPS Publication, Opinion 7/2015.

Privacy by default is a key component of the GDPR framework. Contrarily, the CCPA focuses on adding a layer of transparency to California's data-related economic activity and informing its users of their data rights. Some other state versions of CCPA are the Virginia state's VCDPA and California state's CPRA.[196] After the Consumer Privacy Act was released in 2020, the Privacy Rights Act was released under CCPA (2023) and The Consumer Data Protection Act was released under VCDPA (2023).

Because businesses that operate in this industry rely significantly on processing personal data to offer customers individualized products, the impact of privacy legislation on the value created in the online advertising industry is likely to be significant[197].

Regarding the financial regulations, for businesses in the financial sector, specific regulations like Sarbanes-Oxley[198] or Basel III[199] stipulate how data must be managed, safeguarded, and reported. These rules help to mitigate risks and ensure the integrity of financial markets.

---

196. NIST. 2021. X Marks the Spot. Using Privacy Framework Regulatory Crosswalks to Integrate Compliance and Risk Management. National Institute of Standard and Technology. 2021, U.S. Department of Commerce. Available at: https://www.nist.gov/system/files/documents/2021/12/09/NIST%20Privacy%20Framework%20Webinar%20Presentation%20Deck%20on%2012-2.pdf (last accessed on February 2024).

197. Skiera, B., Miller, K., Jin, Y. 2022. The impact of the General Data Protection Regulation (GDPR) on the online advertising market. Bernd Skiera; 2022.

198. Hurley-Hanson, A.E., Giannantonio, C.M. 2008. Sarbanes oxley act of 2002: Implications for complying corporations. Corporate Ownership and Control 5(3):279-283. DOI:10.22495/cocv5i3c2p3

199. Howard, C. 2014. Basel III's Corporate Governance Impact: How Increased Banking Regulations Pose Challenges to Corporate Compliance While Simultaneously Furthering Stakeholder Objectives. Journal of Business Systems Governance and Ethics (2014) 9(1) JBSGE 39.

It is important to point out that emerging technologies are presenting challenges to traditional regulatory models[200]. One such challenge is the fluidity of data, which can easily cross borders, making it tricky to determine which jurisdiction's laws apply. In the U.S., the Code of Federal Regulations serves as a primary source for various federal rules, including those affecting data analytics. It's a living document that evolves to incorporate new technological advancements.

Some of the best practices for ensuring the compliance with the formal regulations are:

- **Mind the quality of your data management:** Ensure your data is of high quality by using robust data models. It helps not only in meeting compliance standards but also in generating business value.[201]

- **Regular audits:** Carry out periodic audits to ensure that your data handling practices align with current regulations.

- **Stay updated:** Laws and regulations are continuously evolving. Keep yourself updated with the latest amendments to avoid any future mishaps.
Regulatory frameworks in data analytics are not just hoops to jump through; they're essential guidelines that protect both businesses and individuals. So, while they may seem cumbersome, they are instrumental in creating a more ethical and secure data landscape. By following these rules

200. Friedewald, M., Wright, D., Gutwirthcand, S., Mordini, E. 2010. Privacy, data protection and emerging sciences and technologies: towards a common framework. Innovation -The European Journal of Social Science Research, Vol. 23, No. 1, March 2010, 61-67. DOI:10.1080/13511611003791182.

201. La Fever, G. 2017. Meeting Upcoming GDPR Requirements While Maximizing the Full Value of Data Analytics. International Association of Privacy Professionals (IAPP), SSRN Electronic Journal.

and best practices, you're not just following the law; you're contributing to a culture of integrity and trust in the field of data analytics.

7.4 Future of Ethics and Privacy in Data Analytics

Although algorithms and data-driven technology provide us with many advantages, the issue of ethics and privacy still remains a source of potential problems in the near future.

The moral landscape

First of all, the moral landscape is expanding. In a data-driven society, we interact more and more with machines and algorithms. The emerging ethical conundrums are exciting. How much information about us, for instance, should an algorithm be given access to? In order to address the ethical implications of data generation, storage, and consumption, the idea of "data ethics" has emerged[202].

The new frontier of data privacy

In the era of big data, privacy is not only a problem but also a basic right. With increasingly sophisticated data analytics technologies comes a higher risk of privacy infringement. What information should be collected ethically, we must ask ourselves. Who has the authority to examine it? The GDPR in Europe is a start, but there needs to be a global standard[203].

---

202. Floridi, L., Taddeo, M. 2016. What is data ethics? Philosophical Transactions of The Royal Society A Mathematical Physical and Engineering Sciences. 374(2083):20160360. DOI:10.1098/rsta.2016.0360.

203. Mishra, N. 2020. International Trade Law Meets Data Ethics: A Brave New World. New York University Journal of International Law and Politics (Vol 53:2, pages 305-74), ANU College of Law Research Paper No. 21.15.

Frameworks and certifications for ethics

Expect to see firms giving certificates for ethical data practices in the near future. Similar to how they currently do with organic or Fair-Trade labels, businesses will proudly display these. These frameworks will not only provide guidelines for the appropriate use of data but also serve as a benchmark for consumers.

Machine learning and AI

Another level of ethical complexity has been added by the development of AI and machine learning. For instance, it has been demonstrated that racial prejudice exists in predictive policing algorithms[204]. It is the responsibility of data scientists to make sure that algorithms are morally and practically sound.

Ethical data sharing

When it comes to sharing user data without specific authorization, data sharing between businesses can be tricky. More stringent ethical standards for data sharing may necessitate external audits to verify compliance.

The human dimension

In the future, data science education will place more emphasis on human values and empathy. It will be just as important to comprehend the effects of data on human lives as it will be to comprehend the data itself.

Consumer awareness

Consumers will probably be more knowledgeable and cautious about their data in the not-too-distant future. Businesses will need to be open about how they use customer data, possibly integrating

---

204. Hung, T.-W., Yen, C.-P., 2022. Predictive policing and algorithmic fairness. Synthese (2023) 201:206 https://doi.org/10.1007/s11229-023-04189-0.

this information into their product interfaces so that customers can see it right away.

Governmental rules

Last but not least, government rules will have a big impact on how ethical data analytics is done. Different models, ranging from rigid regulatory frameworks to more flexible, market-driven approaches, may be adopted by nations.

So what can we anticipate? In the future, data analytics will be ethical and respectful of personal information in addition to being smart. Everyone has a part to play in this continuing journey, including data scientists, policymakers, and you. The good news is that as we become more aware of these problems, a future that is not only technologically advanced but also morally responsible begins to emerge.

Quiz

1. **Which of the following is NOT a key ethical debate in data analytics?**

    a. The human factor in the analysis process

    b. Privacy and consent

    c. Algorithmic discrimination

    d. The use of automated techniques

2. **Which of the following is NOT an important ethical consideration in data privacy?**

    a. Appropriate anonymization procedures

    b. Secure data storage

    c. The use of personal data only with informed consent

    d. The use of data analytics tools

3. **Which of the following is an example of algorithmic discrimination?**

    a. An algorithm that predicts which customers are most likely to default on a loan

    b. An algorithm that recommends products to customers based on their past purchases

    c. An algorithm that determines which news stories are most likely to be clicked on by users

    d. An algorithm that classifies images of cats and dogs

4. **Which of the following is the best way to mitigate algorithmic discrimination?**

   a. Create algorithms with fairness in mind.

   b. Continuously check the output of algorithms for indications of bias.

   c. Recalibrate algorithms as necessary to encourage fair and equal results.

   d. All of the above

5. **Which of the following is NOT a way to ensure that data is handled responsibly and ethically?**

   a. Use appropriate anonymization procedures.

   b. Secure data storage.

   c. Use personal data only with informed consent.

   d. Share data with other organizations without their knowledge or consent.

6. **What is one of the key advantages of data analytics in marketing?**

   a. Improving data encryption

   b. Reducing operational costs

   c. Enhancing marketing strategies

   d. Improving data collection methods

7. **What are the three major privacy concerns mentioned in the text?**

    a. Data encryption, data redundancy, data sharing

    b. Improper data collection, insufficient data security, unethical use of data

    c. Data availability, data durability, data reliability

    d. Data standardization, data optimization, data visualization

8. **What does the term "privacy by design" refer to?**

    a. The aesthetic aspects of privacy

    b. Implementing privacy measures at the end of the data analytics process

    c. The General Data Protection Regulation (GDPR)

    d. Implementing privacy measures early in the data analytics process

9. **Why are the rules of data privacy changing?**

    a. Because companies are collecting less data

    b. Because people are becoming more aware of the value of their personal data

    c. Because the General Data Protection Regulation (GDPR) has been revoked

    d. Because of the decline in the use of data analytics

10. According to the text, which of the following is most important for companies to succeed in the landscape of data analytics?

    a. Collecting as much data as possible

    b. Ignoring privacy concerns

    c. Respecting privacy as a fundamental human right

    d. Focusing solely on operational efficiency

Answers	1 – d	2 – d	3 – a	4 – d	5 – d
	6 – c	7 – b	8 – d	9 – b	10 – c

Chapter Summary

◆ Some crucial ethical problems relate to: the human factor, privacy and consent, discrimination and fairness;

◆ There are three significant privacy concerns: improper data collection methods, insufficient data security, and the unethical use of data;

◆ There are 2 main types of regulations: data privacy laws (GDPR in Europe, CCPA in the U.S. and the PIPL in China) and financial regulations (like Sarbanes-Oxley or Basel III);

◆ Some of the best practices for ensuring the compliance with the formal regulations are: mind the quality of your Data Management, have regular audits and stay updated;

◆ To future of ethics and privacy issues in data analytics will imply the following: an expanding moral landscape, privacy will become a basic right, firms will start giving certificates for ethical data practices, the development of AI and machine learning will increase the risk of racial prejudices in predictive algorithms and this must be mitigated, there will be an increased need for external audits for controlling the ethics of data sharing, data science education will place more emphasis on human values and empathy, consumers will become more aware of their data privacy, governments will adopt more rules concerning ethical and privacy aspects of data.

Chapter 8

Real-World Case Studies on Data Analytics

Data has been described as the "new oil" of the modern day, with firms utilizing it to obtain insights, streamline processes, and soar to new heights. The range of data's applications in businesses grows along with its volume. This chapter focuses on three unique yet enlightening case studies.

The key learning objectives of this chapter include the reader's understanding of the following:

- How Walmart employs data analytics to boost sales in the retail industry by better understanding customer preferences and streamlining its supply chain.

- How Netflix's success in the streaming sector comes not only from its content but also from the way it leverages viewer data to suggest new shows and decide what else to produce.

- How data analytics was crucial in the healthcare industry in accelerating clinical trials and enhancing the efficacy and distribution of the Oxford/AstraZeneca COVID-19 vaccine, which ultimately resulted in lifesaving measures.

Through these case studies, readers will learn about data analytics' practical applications as well as its technical features, demonstrating how it has the potential to change several industries.

8.1 Case Study 1: Walmart - Transforming Retail through Data Analytics

One of the largest retailers in the world, Walmart, has transformed its inventory management using data analytics. We'll look at how Walmart has maintained its efficiency, competitiveness, and responsiveness to customer needs using data-driven tactics.

Let's first understand Walmart's scale before diving into the specifics. It takes skill to effectively manage inventory with over 11,000 outlets across more than 25 countries, selling about 140,000 products in its supercenters, and having more than 35 million daily customers[205]. To satisfy local demand and avoid extra inventory that can result in waste and higher expenses, Walmart must make sure that each shop is adequately stocked.

205. Dekimpe, M.G. 2020. Retailing and retailing research in the age of big data analytics. ELSEVIER, International Journal of Research in Marketing, Volume 37, Issue 1, March 2020, Pages 3-14, https://doi.org/10.1016/j.ijresmar.2019.09.001 .

In the past, shopkeepers managed their inventory using hand counts, information from previous sales, and their instincts. This strategy frequently resulted in situations of stockouts (missing key supplies) or overstocks (money locked up in unsold goods). Profits and customer confidence could be severely harmed by ineffective inventory management.

Walmart has modernized conventional procedures by integrating big data analytics into its inventory management. To estimate demand with astounding accuracy, sophisticated analytics technologies sift through enormous volumes of data, including weather trends and sales data[206]. With this technology, it is possible to foresee which goods will be in demand where and when, and in what quantities. Additionally, it has assisted Walmart in streamlining its supply chain, enhancing its responsiveness and agility.

Walmart uses machine learning algorithms to change inventory levels on the fly[207]. To predict the requirement for inventory, these algorithms consider a variety of variables, such as seasonal demand, regional events, and even social media mood.

Walmart can make decisions right away thanks to real-time analytics[208]. For instance, the system can redirect extra supplies to the store if a specific item sells off the shelves faster than expected.

206. Singh, M., Rashid, M., Aesaan, M. 2017. Walmart's Sales Data Analysis- A Big Data Analytics Perspective. Conference Proceedings: 2017 4th Asia-Pacific World Congress on Computer Science and Engineering (APWC on CSE), DOI:10.1109/APWConCSE.2017.00028.

207. Singh, M., Rashid, M., Aesaan, M. 2017. Walmart's Sales Data Analysis- A Big Data Analytics Perspective. Conference Proceedings: 2017 4th Asia-Pacific World Congress on Computer Science and Engineering (APWC on CSE), DOI:10.1109/APWConCSE.2017.00028.

208. Bridkmsn, D. 2023. Building Real-Time Analytics Applications. O'Reilly Media, 978-1-098-14656-6, 2023.

Through agility, stockouts are avoided, and customer happiness is increased.

 Walmart uses data analytics to forecast regional product demand based on real-time sales data, local events, and weather forecasts, improving its supply chain and consumer happiness[209]. To ensure that stores fulfill demand effectively, they allow the merchant to alter inventory, such as increasing stockpiles of water and air conditioners during heatwaves. This tactic increases sales and fosters customer loyalty while reducing stockouts.

To promote a cooperative partnership that is advantageous to both parties, Walmart shares its inventory analytics with suppliers[210]. Vendors can modify production plans thanks to real-time data, which lowers lead times and inventory holding costs.

Walmart has improved both the in-store experience and its inventory through data analytics. Walmart has modified store layouts by studying customer behavior to reduce crowding and increase product discoverability.

Walmart continues to test the limits of data analytics, from using IoT devices for real-time shelf monitoring to experimenting with drone technology for inventory scanning[211]. The business is

209. Singh, M., Rashid, M., Aesaan, M. 2017. Walmart's Sales Data Analysis - A Big Data Analytics Perspective. Conference: 2017 4th Asia-Pacific World Congress on Computer Science and Engineering (APWC on CSE). DOI:10.1109/APWConCSE.2017.00028.

210. Liu, X. 2022. Demonstration of Supply Chain Management in Big Data Analysis from Walmart, Toyota, and Amazon. BCP Business & Management 34:1198-1203, DOI:10.54691/bcpbm.v34i.3159.

211. Ivankova, G.V. et al. 2020. Internet of Things (IoT) in logistics. IOP Conference Series: Materials Science and Engineering, 940 012033, doi:10.1088/1757-899X/940/1/012033.

establishing the benchmark for what is feasible in terms of retail inventory management using data analytics.

Walmart's approach to inventory management has been transformed by data analytics, becoming more precise, effective, and economical. Walmart can anticipate customer requirements, work more effectively with suppliers, and ultimately keep its position as the industry leader in retail by making wise use of data.

There you have it, then! Keep this in mind the next time you're in a Walmart and discover exactly what you were looking for: it's not magic; it's the amazing work of data analytics.

8.2 Case Study 2: Netflix Recommendation System

The most popular streaming service in the world, Netflix, is a great example of a business that has successfully used data analytics for marketing.

Netflix is a streaming service available by subscription that provides movies, TV series, and original content. Reed Hastings and Marc Randolph created it in 1997, and Los Gatos, California, serves as the location of its corporate headquarters. In the beginning, Netflix provided DVD rentals via mail, but in 2007 it transitioned to streaming[212]. By changing its business strategy, Netflix was able to cut its losses and increase the number of its subscribers.

---

212. Maddodi, S., Prasad, K. 2019. Netflix Bigdata Analytics - The Emergence of Data Driven Recommendation. International Journal of Case Studies in Business, IT, and Education (IJCSBE), 3(2), 41-51. DOI: org/10.5281/zenodo.3510316.

Over 148 million people are subscribed to Netflix, and it has operations in over 190 countries. The foundation of Netflix's business strategy is subscriptions. To access Netflix's programming, users must pay a monthly fee. Basic, Standard, and Premium are the three distinct Netflix subscription packages available. Both the number of devices that may stream material simultaneously and the streaming quality vary amongst the plans.

According to Maddodi et al. (2019), competition from rival streaming services like Hulu, Disney+, and Amazon Prime Video is becoming more and more intense for the corporation. Netflix is making significant investments in data analytics and machine learning to keep ahead of the competition. The corporation uses these technologies to enhance its recommendation algorithms, which keep subscribers interested.

Netflix invests heavily in data analytics and machine learning to combat some of its challenges: maintaining current users and gaining new ones, expanding subscriber count, increased competition from rival streaming providers, and rising costs of generating original content. Additionally, the business is expanding internationally and creating more unique content.

As one of the first companies to use big data analytics, Netflix issued a challenge in 2006 offering a $1 million prize to anyone who could enhance their current Cinematch recommendation algorithm by 10%[213]. The challenge was to create an algorithm to forecast subscriber movie preferences based on previous data. For roughly 17 thousand movies, Netflix offered a dataset with about 100 million ratings from 480 thousand users. The ratings were

---

213. Bell, R.M, Koren, Y. 2007. Lessons from the Netflix prize challenge. ACM SIGKDD Explorations Newsletter,9(2):75–79, 2007.

provided in the form of user, movie name, date of rating, and user-provided rating.[214]

The contest went on for several years, and in 2008 BellKor's Pragmatic Chaos team, which included mathematicians, data scientists, and engineers from various countries, industries, and research institutes like AT&T, Yahoo, Commendo Research, & Consulting GmbH, was given the prize. Netflix's recommendation systems make use of data science and big data analytics. The phrase "recommender system" was first used in information system literature in the late 1990s.[215] The popularity of the recommendation system is still high since it is used to effectively address a variety of business problems. Several companies, like Amazon, Microsoft, etc. use a commercial recommendation system.[216]

Netflix's recommendation system uses machine learning to suggest content based on subscribers' interests. It gathers user data, including location, watched content, interests, search data, and viewing time. The system's algorithm uses these inputs to offer personalized recommendations. Primarily, it values user profiles, which hold information like subscriber interests, search history, and interactions. When creating a new profile or account, Netflix prompts subscribers to select genres or titles as initial recommendation parameters. If ignored, Netflix displays popular content. The system adjusts recommendations based on viewed

214. Maddodi, S., Prasad, K. 2019. Netflix Bigdata Analytics - The Emergence of Data Driven Recommendation. International Journal of Case Studies in Business, IT, and Education (IJCSBE), 3(2), 41-51. DOI: org/10.5281/zenodo.3510316.

215. Resnick, P., Varian, H. 1997. Recommender systems. Commun.ACM30(3):56-58.

216. Linden, G., Smith, B., York, J. 2003. Amazon.com Recommendations: Item-to-Item Collaborative Filtering. Published by the IEEE Computer Society, IEEE InternetComput. 7(1):76-80.

content, prioritizing recent viewing habits over initial preferences provided by the subscriber.[217]

Recommendation systems primarily use two methods[218]:

1. **Content-based filtering:** this method suggests content based on the subscriber's past behavior. A user will be offered more content in the same categories if they have previously loved comedy or action.

2. **Collaborative filtering:** Based on user profiles that are similar.[219] The recommendation system primarily considers subscriber preferences and history while building a subscriber profile. For instance, if subscriber A likes crime, action, and horror films while subscriber B enjoys crime, action, and comedy films, then subscriber A is also likely to choose comedy films while subscriber B will also prefer horror films.

---

217. Carlos, A., Uribe, G., Hunt, N. 2015. The Netflix recommender system: Algorithms, business value, and innovation. ACM Trans. Manage. Inf. Syst. 6, 4, Article 13 (December 2015), 19 pages. DOI: http://dx.doi.org/10.1145/2843948 .

218. Adomavicius, G., Tuzhilin, A. 2005. Toward the Next Generation of Recommender Systems: A Survey of the State-of-the-Art and Possible Extensions. IEEETrans. Knowl. Data Eng. 17(6):734-749.

219. Balabanovic, M., Shoham Y. 1997. FAB: Content-based, Collaborative Recommendation. Communications of the Association for Computing Machinery 40(3) (1997) 66-72.

The difference between the two can be seen in Figure 8.1.

| Figure 8.1 | **Recommendation Technique** |

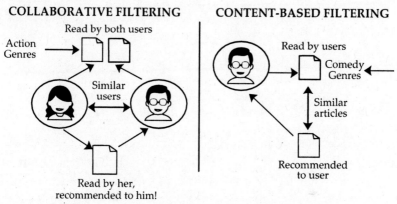

COLLABORATIVE FILTERING   CONTENT-BASED FILTERING

Source: Maddodi, S., Prasad, K. 2019. Netflix Bigdata Analytics - The Emergence of Data-Driven Recommendation. International Journal of Case Studies in Business, IT, and Education (IJCSBE), 3(2), 41-51. DOI: org/10.5281/zenodo.3510316.

The techniques Netflix uses will change as the market and technology change. They are constantly looking for novel approaches to better understand their consumers and provide them with engaging content. The cycle of listening, picking up knowledge, and applying it never ends.

Fun Fact

Eighty percent of the content viewed on Netflix originates from suggestions made by the platform's highly sophisticated recommendation system, as opposed to direct searches[220]. By decreasing churn and retaining users with the material they enjoy, this method effectively shapes not only viewing habits but also production decisions, saving Netflix an estimated $1 billion annually.

Finally, Netflix's skillful application of data analytics serves as an example of the revolutionary potential of data in the current digital era. They'll probably continue to lead the streaming market as long as they take advantage of these insights, always prepared to release the next smash hit that gets everyone tweeting.

8.3 Case Study 3: Improving Healthcare Outcomes with Data Analytics – the Oxford/ AstraZeneca COVID-19 vaccine

The use of data analytics in healthcare has enabled previously unheard-of improvements across many medical specialties, particularly in terms of improving healthcare outcomes, but also in reducing costs and increasing patient satisfaction. The use of data analytics to evaluate the risks related to the Oxford/ AstraZeneca COVID-19 vaccine was one example of a significant integration.

---

220. Pajkovic, N. 2022. Algorithms and taste-making: Exposing the Netflix Recommender System's operational logics. Convergence: The International Journal of Research into New Media Technologies, Vol. 28(1) 214–235. DOI: 10.1177/13548565211014464.

Data Analytics in the healthcare industry is based on using massive data reservoirs, such as patient records and clinical trials, to inform decision-making processes.

The scientific world was under extreme pressure to create an efficient vaccine in a short amount of time because of the global epidemic. One of the front-runners was the Oxford/AstraZeneca vaccine, which in preliminary testing had encouraging efficacy rates. However, it was crucial to comprehend its hazards, just like with any drugs and vaccines.

In mid-March 2021, a number of nations halted the introduction of the Oxford-AstraZeneca COVID-19 vaccination over worries that the shot could cause thrombosis and thrombocytopenia[221]. Many others cautioned that this would undermine public confidence at a crucial time for the pandemic response.

Vaccines go through extensive research in phase I and phase II clinical trials to determine their efficacy and safety prior to being approved by the appropriate authorities[222]. The vaccine-related immunopathology that develops in vaccinated individuals during a natural illness is one specific safety concern[223].

The COVID-19 vaccinations were used once clinical trials showed that they are effective and safe. However, research

---

221. Jain, V., Lorgelly, P., 2021. The impact of pausing the Oxford-AstraZeneca COVID-19 vaccine on uptake in Europe: a difference-in-differences analysis. European Journal of Public Health. Doi: 10.1093/eurpub/ckac039.

222. Yesuf, E.A. et al. 2022. Self-reported side effects of the Oxford AstraZeneca COVID-19 vaccine among healthcare workers in Ethiopia, Africa: A cross-sectional study. Public Health, 19 July 2022, Sec. Infectious Diseases, Surveillance, Prevention and Treatment, Volume 10 - 2022 | https://doi.org/10.3389/fpubh.2022.937794.

223. Su, S., Du, L. 2021. Learning from the past: development of safe and effective COVID-19 vaccines. Nat Rev Microbiol. 19:211–9. doi: 10.1038/s41579-020-00462-y.

should be done on the long-term effects. The safety of COVID-19 vaccinations can be investigated using a variety of techniques. Active and passive surveillance are a couple of the tools[224]. Active surveillance, a proactive strategy of actively identifying and monitoring cases that frequently involve medical personnel informing authorities about certain diseases, is available mostly in industrialized countries. Passive surveillance, in contrast, analyzes cases through cross-sectional research, and the cases are reported voluntarily.

However, the mere existence of more data is of no use to public health unless it can be used to generate "actionable data" that will lead to better health outcomes and more effective and efficient health systems[225]. And this is where data analytics comes into play.

Using analytics on the Oxford-AstraZeneca COVID-19 vaccination, the following revelations were made:

- Only a very small percentage of recipients had problems with blood clotting[226].

- Individualized vaccination tactics were required due to the diverse responses of certain populations, such as age and gender.

- The majority of side effects were minor and transient, and for the majority of the population, the advantages of vaccination outweigh the risks. However, as a precaution,

224. Petousis-Harris, H. 2020. Assessing the safety of COVID-19 vaccines: a primer. Drug Safety. (2020) 43:1205–10. doi: 10.1007/s40264-020-01002-6.

225. Leyens, L., Reumann, M., Malats, N., Brand, A. 2017. Use of big data for drug development and for public and personal health and care. Genet Epidemiol. (2017) 41:51–60. doi: 10.1002/gepi.22012.

226. Wise, J. 2021. Covid-19: Rare immune response may cause clots after AstraZeneca vaccine. BMJ 2021; 373 doi: https://doi.org/10.1136/bmj.n954.

some nations only allowed particular age groups to receive the vaccine.

Adaptive tactics, such as modifying the vaccination dosage or combining it with other vaccines, were made possible by real-time data analysis.

This event established a standard. The Oxford/AstraZeneca vaccine's quick and effective risk assessment demonstrates the potential of data analytics in upcoming vaccine advancements and other medical breakthroughs. It demonstrates the effectiveness of data-driven choices in improving results in the world of healthcare.

To sum up, the application of data analytics in healthcare goes beyond simple technological development. It is a paradigm shift that ensures continuous medical decisions are supported by considerable and continuously evolving data rather than merely relying on a small number of trials or intuitions. A beacon, the Oxford/AstraZeneca COVID-19 vaccination risk assessment illuminates the way for upcoming medical advancements and tactics.

Quiz

1. **Walmart, known as one of the largest retailers, has revamped its inventory management through what means?**

    a. Manual counting

    b. Hiring more employees

    c. Data analytics

    d. Installing more shelves

2. **How many products does Walmart sell in its supercenters?**

    a. Over 11,000 products

    b. About 140,000 products

    c. More than 25,000 products

    d. Less than 100,000 products

3. **Walmart utilizes which kind of algorithms to adjust inventory levels?**

    a. Binary algorithms

    b. Quantum algorithms

    c. Machine learning algorithms

    d. Sorting algorithms

4. What can real-time analytics enable Walmart to do?

    a. Predict future global events

    b. Increase product prices instantly

    c. Take decisions immediately

    d. Increase product production

5. How has Walmart improved the in-store experience?

    a. By offering discounts to loyal customers

    b. By introducing more checkout counters

    c. By modifying store layouts based on customer behavior

    d. By playing soothing music in the store

6. What is Netflix's primary business strategy?

    a. Subscriptions

    b. Advertising

    c. DVD rentals

    d. Producing original content

7. What two challenges is Netflix facing?

    a. Maintaining current users and gaining new ones

    b. Increased competition from rival streaming providers

    c. Rising costs of generating original content

    d. All of the above

8. **What is the purpose of the Netflix Cinematch recommendation algorithm?**

   a. To predict subscriber movie preferences based on previous data

   b. To recommend new movies to subscribers based on their interests

   c. To improve the quality of Netflix's streaming service

   d. To reduce Netflix's costs

9. **What are the two main methods used by recommendation systems?**

   a. Content-based filtering and collaborative filtering

   b. Machine learning and deep learning

   c. Natural language processing and computer vision

   d. Regression and classification

10. **What is the main lesson we can learn from Netflix's use of data analytics?**

    a. Data can be used to improve all aspects of a business.

    b. It is important to invest in data analytics and machine learning.

    c. Data can be used to better understand customers and provide them with engaging content.

    d. All of the above

Answers	1 – c	2 – b	3 – c	4 – c	5 – c
	6 – a	7 – d	8 – a	9 – a	10 – d

Chapter Summary

◆ Data has been called the "new oil" of the current business world, with companies using it to gain fresh insights, optimize workflows, and reach unprecedented heights.

◆ Three distinct yet insightful case studies highlight the transformative potential of data analytics in a variety of businesses: Walmart, Netflix, and the risk assessment regarding the Oxford/AstraZeneca COVID-19 vaccine.

◆ Walmart, one of the world's leading retailers, has revolutionized its inventory management by integrating data analytics, enabling precise demand predictions, optimizing the supply chain, and enhancing customer experience.

◆ Innovations in retail include real-time analytics for immediate decision-making, machine learning for inventory adjustments, collaboration with suppliers using shared data, or experimentation with IoT and drone technology for inventory management.

◆ Netflix uses data analytics to personalize its recommendations for each subscriber, making it more likely that they will find something they want to watch.

◆ Also, data analytics is used in Netflix to target its marketing campaigns to specific groups of subscribers, based on their interests and viewing habits.

◆ Data analytics in healthcare utilizes vast data sources like patient records and clinical trials, enabling major improvements in healthcare outcomes. This was evident in the evaluation of the Oxford/AstraZeneca COVID-19 vaccine, where analytics revealed that only a small percentage of recipients had severe side effects and helped guide individualized vaccination strategies.

◆ The Oxford/AstraZeneca COVID-19 vaccine's risk assessment, driven by data analytics, represents a shift in healthcare. This shift emphasizes decisions based on extensive, evolving data over solely relying on limited trials or intuition, showcasing the potential of data analytics for future medical advancements and strategies.

Data analytics is a game-changer in a variety of industries. With the use of big data and machine learning, the area has advanced from its modest beginnings to its current capabilities, which enable accurate insights for decision-making. Businesses will need to continually adapt and make strategic investments as the use of machine learning and artificial intelligence in data analytics increases.

Glossary

This glossary defines key terms used throughout the book, offering readers clarity on important concepts and jargon in the field of data analytics.

Algorithm – A set of mathematical instructions or rules that, especially if given to a computer, will help to calculate an answer to a problem.

Analytics – The systematic computational analysis of data or statistics.

Big data – Large and complex data sets that traditional data-processing application software is inadequate to deal with.

Classification – A data analysis task, i.e., the process of finding a model (or function) that describes and distinguishes data classes or concepts.

Clustering – The task of grouping a set of objects in such a way that objects in the same group are more similar to each other than to those in other groups.

Data Collection – A process in which information is gathered and expressed in a summary form for statistical analysis.

Data Cleaning – The process of detecting and correcting (or removing) corrupt or inaccurate records from a record set, table, or database.

Data Integration – The process of combining data from different sources into a single, unified view.

Data Mining – The process of sorting through large data sets to identify patterns and establish relationships to solve problems.

Data Modeling – The process of establishing a specific data model for a determined problem domain.

Data Quality – The state of qualitative or quantitative pieces of information.

Data Visualization – The graphic representation of data.

Database – A structured set of data held in a computer, especially one that is accessible in various ways.

Deep Learning – Part of a broader family of machine learning methods based on artificial neural networks with representation learning.

Descriptive Analytics – The interpretation of historical data to better understand changes that have occurred in a business.

Forecasting – The process of making predictions of the future based on past and present data.

Inferential Statistics – Producing, interpreting, and validating conclusions from data subject to random variation.

Machine Learning – A type of artificial intelligence that allows software applications to become more accurate at predicting outcomes without being explicitly programmed to do so.

Metadata – Data that provides information about other data.

Normalization – The process of organizing the columns and tables of a relational database to minimize data redundancy.

Predictive Analytics – The practice of extracting information from existing data sets to determine patterns and predict future outcomes and trends.

Prescriptive Analytics – The area of business analytics dedicated to finding the best course of action for a given situation.

Quantitative Data – Data expressing a certain quantity, amount, or range.

Query – A request for data or information from a database table or combination of tables.

Regression Analysis – A statistical process for estimating the relationships among variables.

Sentiment Analysis – The process of computationally identifying and categorizing opinions expressed in a piece of text.

Structured Data – Data that resides in fixed fields within a record or file or is organized in a defined manner.

Time Series Analysis – The analysis of ordered sequential data, either to extract meaningful statistics or to predict future points in the series (forecasting).

Unstructured Data – Information that either does not have a pre-defined data model or is not organized in a pre-defined manner. Unstructured information is typically text-heavy but may contain data such as dates, numbers, and facts.

Bibliography

Adomavicius, G., Tuzhilin, A. 2005. Toward the Next Generation of Recommender Systems: A Survey of the State-of-the-Art and Possible Extensions. IEEETrans. Knowl. Data Eng. 17(6):734-749.

Ajah, I.A., Nweke, H.F. 2019. Big Data and Business Analytics: Trends, Platforms, Success Factors and Applications. Big Data Cogn. Comput. 2019, 3(2), 32; https://doi.org/10.3390/bdcc3020032.

Akobeng, A. 2016. Understanding type I and type II errors, statistical power and sample size. 2016 Foundation Acta Pædiatrica. Published by John Wiley & Sons Ltd. https://doi.org/10.1111/apa.13384.

Alasadi, S.A., Bhaya, W.S. 2017. Review of Data Preprocessing Techniques in Data Mining. Journal of Engineering and Applied Sciences 12(16): 4102-4107. ISBN: 1816-949X.

Ardagna, C.A., Bellandi, V., Damiani, E., Bezzi, M., Hebert, C. 2021. Big Data Analytics-as-a-Service: Bridging the gap between security experts and data scientists. Computers & Electrical Engineering, Volume 93, July 2021, 107215.

Asri, H, 2015. Big Data in healthcare: Challenges and Opportunities. Big Data in healthcare: Challenges and Opportunities, 1, 1-5.

Baesens, B. 2014. Analytics in a Big Data World: The Essential Guide to Data Science and its Applications. Willey, ISBN: 9781118892701.

Balabanovic, M., Shoham Y. 1997. FAB: Content-based, Collaborative Recommendation. Communications of the Association for Computing Machinery 40(3) (1997) 66-72.

Banarescu, A. 2015. Detecting and Preventing Fraud with Data Analytics. Procedia Economics and Finance 32 (2015) 1827 – 1836. DOI: 10.1016/S2212-5671(15)01485-9.

Balachandran, B.M., Prasad, S. 2017. Challenges and Benefits of Deploying Big Data Analytics in the Cloud for Business Intelligence. Procedia Computer Science, Volume 112, 2017, Pages 1112-1122.

Banik, A., Bandyopadhyay, S.K. 2016. Big Data-A Review on Analysing 3Vs. Journal of Scientific and Engineering Research, 2016, 3(1). ISSN: 2394-2630.

Barrech, K. et al. 2020. IOM Monitoring and Evaluation Guidelines. International Organization for Migration (IOM), Geneva. ISBN 978-92-9268-016-9.

Baumer, B., Garcia, R.L., Kim, A.Y., Kinnaird, K.M., Ott, M.Q. 2022. Integrating Data Science Ethics Into an Undergraduate Major: A Case Study. Taylor & Francis Group, Journal of Statistics and Data Science Education, Volume 30, 2022, Issue 1, DOI: https://doi.org/10.1080/26939169.2022.2038041 .

Bell, R.M, Koren, Y. 2007. Lessons from the Netflix prize challenge. ACM SIGKDD Explorations Newsletter,9(2):75–79, 2007.

Berinato, S. 2016. Visualizations That Really Work. Published in Harvard Business Review, June 2016: Managing the 24/7 Workplace.

Bhattacherjee, A. 2012. Social science research: Principles, methods, and practices (2nd ed.). Textbooks Collection 3. Tampa Library at Digital Commons @ University of South Florida. https://digitalcommons.usf.edu/oa_textbooks/3.

Bibri, S.E., Krogstie, J. 2017. The core enabling technologies of big data analytics and context-aware computing for smart sustainable cities: a review and synthesis. Journal of Big Data 4, 38 (2017). https://doi.org/10.1186/s40537-017-0091-6 .

Biswas, A., Dutta, S., Turton, T.L., Ahrens, J. 2022. Sampling for Scientific Data Analysis and Reduction. In: Childs, H., Bennett, J.C., Garth, C. (eds) In Situ Visualization for Computational Science. Mathematics and Visualization. Springer, Cham. DOI: https://doi.org/10.1007/978-3-030-81627-8_2 .

Bonthu, Sridevi, and K Hima Bindu. 2017. Review of Leading Data Analytics Tools. International Journal of Engineering & Technology, 7 (3.31) 10-15.

Bormida, Marina Da. 2021. The Big Data World: Benefits, Threats and Ethical Challenges. Iphofen, R. and O'Mathúna, D. (Ed.) Ethical Issues in Covert, Security and Surveillance Research (Advances in Research Ethics and Integrity, Vol. 8, Emerald Publishing Limited, Bingley 71-91.

Bridkmsn, D. 2023. Building Real-Time Analytics Applications. O'Reilly Media, 978-1-098-14656-6, 2023.

Brodie, M.L. 2019. What Is Data Science? Applied Data Science (pp.101-130). DOI:10.1007/978-3-030-11821-1_8 .

Brown, S. 2020. How to build a data-driven company. MIT Management Sloan School. URL: https://mitsloan.mit.edu/ideas-made-to-matter/how-to-build-a-data-driven-company .

Brown, S. 2021. Machine learning, explained. MIT Management Sloan School. URL: https://mitsloan.mit.edu/ideas-made-to-matter/machine-learning-explained .

Bull, P., Centurion, C., Keams, S., Kelso, E. Viswanathan, N. 2017. Prescriptive Analytics for Business Leaders. Independent Publisher. ISBN: 1532357540, 9781532357541.

Carlos, A., Uribe, G., Hunt, N. 2015. The Netflix recommender system: Algorithms, business value, and innovation. ACM Trans. Manage. Inf. Syst. 6, 4, Article 13 (December 2015), 19 pages. DOI: http://dx.doi.org/10.1145/2843948 .

Chakri, P., Pratap, S., Lakshay, Gouda, S.K. 2023. An exploratory data analysis approach for analyzing financial accounting data using machine learning. Elsevier - Decision Analytics Journal, Volume 7, June 2023, 100212. https://doi.org/10.1016/j.dajour.2023.100212 .

Cham. 2016. Secondary Analysis of Electronic Health Records. MIT Critical Data. Springer, ISBN-13: 978-3-319-43740-8ISBN-13: 978-3-319-43742-2.

ChengXiang Zhai, Sean Massung. 2016. Text Data Management and Analysis: A Practical Introduction to Information Retrieval and Text Mining. Association for Computing Machinery and Morgan & Claypool. DOI: https://doi.org/10.1145/2915031.

Christ, M., Krumeich, J., Kempa-Liehr, A.W. 2016. Integrating predictive analytics into complex event processing by using conditional density estimations. In: IEEE 20th international enterprise distributed object computing workshop (EDOCW). In: IEEE computer society, Los Alamitos, CA, USA; 2016. pp. 1–8. https://doi.org/10.1109/EDOCW.2016.7584363.

Corsi, A., de Souza, F.F., Pagani, R.N. et al. 2021. Big data analytics as a tool for fighting pandemics: a systematic review of literature. Journal of Ambient Intelligence and Humanized Computing 12, 9163–9180 (2021). https://doi.org/10.1007/s12652-020-02617-4 .

Cote, C. 2021. 4 Types of Data Analytics to Improve Decision-Making. Harvard Business School Online. URL: https://online.hbs.edu/blog/post/types-of-data-analysis .

Cousineau, D., Chartier, S. 2010. Outliers detection and treatment: a review. International Journal of Psychological Research, 3 (1), 59-68. ISSN: 2011-2084. DOI: 10.21500/20112084.844.

Cozzoli N, Salvatore FP, Faccilongo N, Milone M. 2022. How can big data analytics be used for healthcare organization management? Literary framework and future research from a systematic review. BMC Health Serv Res. 2022 Jun 22;22(1):809. doi: 10.1186/s12913-022-08167-z. PMID: 35733192; PMCID: PMC9213639.

Darwen, H. 2010. An Introduction to Relational Database Theory. Hugh Darwen & Ventus Publishing ApS, ISBN 978-87-7681-500-4.

Dekera, K., Eke, C.I. 2022. Smart farming prediction models for precision agriculture: a comprehensive survey. Springer, Artificial Intelligence Review. DOI: https://doi.org/10.1007/s10462-022-10266-6.

Dekimpe, M.G. 2020. Retailing and retailing research in the age of big data analytics. ELSEVIER, International Journal of Research in Marketing, Volume 37, Issue 1, March 2020, Pages 3-14, https://doi.org/10.1016/j.ijresmar.2019.09.001 .

Demir, A. 2017. Importance of Data Analysis on Achieving the Organizational Goals during The Short Term Strategic Plan: Case of Service Quality and Students' Satisfaction Level at Ishik University. International Journal of Social Sciences & Educational Studies.ISSN 2520-0968 (Online), ISSN 2409-1294 (Print), March 2017, Vol.3, No.3.

Di Zio, M., Fursova, N., Gelsema, T., Gießing, S., Guarnera, U., Petrauskienė, J., Kalben, L.Q., Scanu, M., Bosch, K.O., van der Loo, M., Walsdorfer, K. 2016. Methodology for Data Validation 1.0. Essnet Validat Foundation. URL: https://cros-legacy.ec.europa.eu/system/files/methodology_for_data_validation_v1.0_rev-2016-06_final.pdf .

Dietrich, D., Heller, B., Yang, B. 2015. Data Science & Big Data Analytics: Discovering, Analyzing, Visualizing and Presenting Data. John Wiley & Sons, Inc. ISBN: 978-1-118-87613-8.

Dodge, Y. 2010. The concise Encyclopedia of Statistics. Springer, New York, NY. https://doi.org/10.1007/978-0-387-32833-1_136.

Dulal, R. 2016. Big Data and Google File System. Proceedings of the Conference: 8th National Students' Conference on Information TechnologyAt: Kathmandu, Nepal.

Dutta, P. 2019. Business Analytics using Microsoft Power BI and AWS Redshift. International Journal of Trend in Scientific Research and Development (IJTSRD), Volume: 3 I Issue: 2 I Jan-Feb 2019 Available Online: www.ijtsrd.com e-ISSN: 2456 - 6470.

EPA. 2023. Exploratory Data Analysis. United States Environmental Protection Agency. URL: https://www.epa.gov/caddis-vol4/exploratory-data-analysis.

European Data Protection Supervisor. 2015. Meeting the challenges of big data. EDPS Publication, Opinion 7/2015.

Fan, J., Han, F., Liu, H. 2014. Challenges of Big Data Analysis. National Science Review, 1:293-324, 2014, https://doi.org/10.1093/nsr/nwt032 .

Fan, C., Wang, J., Chen, M., Wang, X. 2021. A Review on Data Preprocessing Techniques Toward Efficient and Reliable Knowledge Discovery From Building Operational Data. Frontiers in Energy Research, Volume 9, DOI:10.3389/fenrg.2021.652801.

Fangohr, H., Beg, M., Bergemann, M., Bondar, V. 2019. Data exploration and analysis with Jupyter notebooks. Proceedings of The 17th International Conference on Accelerator and Large Experimental Physics Control Systems, New York, NY, USA, DOI: 10.18429/JACoW-ICALEPCS2019-TUCPR02.

Floridi, L., Taddeo, M. 2016. What is data ethics? Philosophical Transactions of The Royal Society A Mathematical Physical and Engineering Sciences. 374(2083):20160360. DOI:10.1098/rsta.2016.0360.

Friedewald, M., Wright, D., Gutwirthcand, S., Mordini, E. 2010. Privacy, data protection and emerging sciences and technologies: towards a common framework. Innovation -The European Journal of Social Science Research, Vol. 23, No. 1, March 2010, 61-67. DOI:10.1080/13511611003791182.

Gallo, A. 2015. A Refresher on Regression Analysis. Harvard Business Review. URL: https://hbr.org/2015/11/a-refresher-on-regression-analysis .

Gantz, D.R.J. 2013. The Digital Universe in 2020: Big Data, Bigger Digital Shadows, and Biggest Growth in the Far East. IDC, 2013.

Garoufallou, E., Gaitanou, P. 2021. Big Data: Opportunities and Challenges in Libraries, a Systematic Literature Review. Association of College & Research Libraries, Vol.82, No.3 (2021). URL: https://crl.acrl.org/index.php/crl/article/view/24918/32769 .

Gauld, A.. 2017. Insight Driven Organisation survey. Report: Benchmarking your analytics journey. Deloitte company report, 2017. Available at: https://www2.deloitte.com/content/dam/Deloitte/uk/Documents/technology/deloitte-uk-tech-ido-survey.pdf

Genc, S.Y. 2021. The Medici's Influence: Revival of Political and Financial Thought in Europe. Belleten, April 2021, DOI: 10.37879/belleten.2021.29.

General Data Protection Regulation (GDPR). Art. 25 GDPR. Data protection by design and by default. General Data Protection Regulation of the European Union, Article 25. URL: https://gdpr-info.eu/art-25-gdpr/ .

Ghosh, S., Neha, K. 2019. Social Media Analytics using Qlik Connectors. International Journal of Recent Technology and Engineering (IJRTE). ISSN: 2277-3878, Volume-8, Issue-2S11, September 2019.

Gudivada, V.N. 2017. Data Analytics for Intelligent Transportation Systems. Elsevier, ISBN 978-0-12-809715-1.

Heiss, Andreas. 2019. Big Data Challenges in Big Science. Computing and Software for Big Science 3, 15 (2019). https://doi.org/10.1007/s41781-019-0030-7 .

Ho, D.A., Beyan, O. 2020. Biases in Data Science Lifecycle. ArXiv. URL: https://arxiv.org/pdf/2009.09795.pdf .

Howard, C. 2014. Basel III's Corporate Governance Impact: How Increased Banking Regulations Pose Challenges to Corporate Compliance While Simultaneously Furthering Stakeholder Objectives. Journal of Business Systems Governance and Ethics (2014) 9(1) JBSGE 39.

Hung, T.-W., Yen, C.-P., 2022. Predictive policing and algorithmic fairness. Synthese (2023) 201:206. https://doi.org/10.1007/s11229-023-04189-0.

Hurley-Hanson, A.E., Giannantonio, C.M. 2008. Sarbanes oxley act of 2002: Implications for complying corporations. Corporate Ownership and Control 5(3):279-283. DOI:10.22495/cocv5i3c2p3.

Institute of Medicine and National Research Council. 2002. Integrity in Scientific Research: Creating an Environment That Promotes Responsible Conduct. Washington, DC: The National Academies Press. https://doi.org/10.17226/10430.

Internet Live Stats. 2023. Google Search Statistics. Internet Live Stats. Retrieved in November 2023 from https://www.internetlivestats.com/google-search-statistics/.

Ivankova, G.V. et al. 2020. Internet of Things (IoT) in logistics. IOP Conference Series: Materials Science and Engineering, 940 012033, doi:10.1088/1757-899X/940/1/012033.

Jain, V., Lorgelly, P. 2021. The impact of pausing the Oxford-AstraZeneca COVID-19 vaccine on uptake in Europe: a difference-in-differences analysis. European Journal of Public Health. Doi: 10.1093/eurpub/ckac039.

Jajuga, K., Sokolowski, A., Bock, H.H. 2002. Classification, Clustering, and Data Analysis. Recent Advances and Applications. Conference Proceedings of The Eighth Conference of the International Federation of Classification Societies (IFCS), 2002.

Jehad, A., Rehanullah, K., Nasir, A. Imran, M. 2012. Random Forests and Decision Trees. IJCSI International Journal of Computer Science Issues, Vol. 9, Issue 5, No 3, September 2012. ISSN (Online): 1694-0814.

Kabir, S.M.S. 2016. Methods of Data Collection. In book: Basic Guidelines for Research: An Introductory Approach for All Disciplines (pp.201-275). Publisher: Book Zone Publication.

Karinshak, E., Jin, Y. 2023. AI-driven disinformation: a framework for organizational preparation and response. Emerald Publishing Limited. Journal of communication management, 23 Oct 2023, Vol. 27, Issue 4, pages 539 - 562. ISSN: 1363254X. DOI: 10.1108/JCOM-09-2022-0113.

Khanra, S., Dhir, A., Islam, A.K.M.N., Mantymaki, M. 2020. Big data analytics in healthcare: a systematic literature review. Journal of Enterprise Information System, Volume 14, 2020 - Issue 7, https://doi.org/10.1080/17517575.2020.1812005 .

Kim, M., Zimmermann, T., DeLine, R., Begel, A. 2016. The Emerging Role of Data Scientists on Software Development Teams. Proceedings of The 2016 IEEE/ACM 38th IEEE International Conference on Software Engineering. DOI: http://dx.doi.org/10.1145/2884781.2884783.

Koltay, T. 2019. Data literacy in academia: Basics and pedagogical views. Opus et Educatio 6(4), DOI:10.3311/ope.343.

Kumar, V. 2018. Predictive Analytics: A Review of Trends and Techniques. International Journal of Computer Applications 182(1):31-37, DOI: 10.5120/ijca2018917434.

La Fever, G. 2017. Meeting Upcoming GDPR Requirements While Maximizing the Full Value of Data Analytics. International Association of Privacy Professionals (IAPP), SSRN Electronic Journal.

Lapatas, V., Stefanidakis, M., Jimenez, R.C. et al. 2015. Data integration in biological research: an overview. Journal of Biological Result-Thessaloniki 22, 9 (2015). DOI: https://doi.org/10.1186/s40709-015-0032-5 .

Lefebvre, H., Legner, C., Fadler, M. 2021. Data democratization: toward a deeper understanding. Proceedings of The Forty-Second International Conference on Information Systems, Austin 2021.

Lepenioti, K., Bousdekis, A., Apostolou, D., Mentzas, G. 2020. Prescriptive analytics: Literature review and research challenges. International Journal of Information Management. Volume 50, February 2020, Pages 57-70.

LeSueur, J. 2012. Data Acquisition, Storage, and Retrieval (Chapter 12). Marketing Automation: Practical Steps to More Effective Direct Marketing. Wiley Online Library. https://doi. org/10.1002/9781119197782.ch12 .

Leyens, L., Reumann, M., Malats, N., Brand, A. 2017. Use of big data for drug development and for public and personal health and care. Genet Epidemiol. (2017) 41:51–60. doi: 10.1002/gepi.22012.

Linden, G., Smith, B., York, J. 2003. Amazon.com Recommendations: Item-to-Item Collaborative Filtering. Published by the IEEE Computer Society, IEEE InternetComput. 7(1):76-80.

Liu, H. 2018. Feature Engineering for Machine Learning and Data Analytics. Chapman & Hall/ CRC Press. ISBN 9780367571856.

Liu, M., Wang, Z., Gong, Z. 2020. Data Exploration. ML - CMU EDU. URL: https://blog.ml.cmu. edu/2020/08/31/2-data-exploration/ .

Liu, X. 2022. Demonstration of Supply Chain Management in Big Data Analysis from Walmart, Toyota, and Amazon. BCP Business & Management 34:1198-1203, DOI:10.54691/bcpbm.v34i.3159.

Long, C. et al. 2015. Data Science & Big Data Analytics: Discovering, Analyzing, Visualizing and Presenting Data. John Wiley & Sons, Inc., Canada. ISBN: 978-1-118-87613-8.

Luan, H., Geczy, P., Lai, H., Gobert, J., Yang, S.J.H., Ogata, H/, Baltes, J., Guerra, R., Li, P., Tsai, C.C. 2020. Challenges and Future Directions of Big Data and Artificial Intelligence in Education. Front Psychol. 2020 Oct 19;11:580820. doi: 10.3389/fpsyg.2020.580820. PMID: 33192896; PMCID: PMC7604529.

Ma, A. 2020. Making Data Reports Useful: From Descriptive to Predictive. National Library of Medicine. Cureus, v.12(10); 2020 October; e10920. URL: https://www.ncbi.nlm.nih.gov/pmc/articles/ PMC7657442/ .

Maddodi, S., Prasad, K. 2019. Netflix Bigdata Analytics - The Emergence of Data Driven Recommendation. International Journal of Case Studies in Business, IT, and Education (IJCSBE), 3(2), 41-51. DOI: org/10.5281/zenodo.3510316.

Maillart, T. 2015. The Extreme Risk of Personal Data Breaches & The Erosion of Privacy. The European Physical Journal B 89(1). DOI:10.1140/epjb/e2015-60754-4 .

Manyika, J., Chui, M., Brown, B., Bughin, J., Dobbs, R., Roxburgh, C., Byer, A.H.. 2011. Big data: The next frontier for innovation, competition, and productivity. McKinsey&Company.

Marczyk, G. R., DeMatteo, D., Festinger, D. 2010. Essentials of research design and methodology (Vol. 2). John Wiley & Sons.

Markham, A. N., Tiidenberg, K., & Herman, A. 2018. Ethics as Methods: Doing Ethics in the Era of Big Data Research—Introduction. Social Media + Society, 4(3). https://doi. org/10.1177/2056305118784502

Maryville's online Bachelor of Science in Data Science. 2023. Data Science vs. Data Analytics: Understanding the Differences. Accessed May 22, 2023. https://online.maryville.edu/blog/data-science-vs-data-analytics/.

Mayor, T. 2023. How to build an effective analytics practice: 7 insights from MIT experts. MIT Management Sloan School. URL: https://mitsloan.mit.edu/ideas-made-to-matter/how-to-build-effective-analytics-practice-7-insights-mit-experts .

McCord, S.E., Karl, J.W., Fults, G., Webb, N.P. 2021. Ten practical questions to improve data quality. Society for Range Management, Rangelands, RALA-00301, DOI: 10.1016/j.rala.2021.07.006.

Mehmood, A., Natgunanathan, I., Xiang, Y., Hua, G., Song, G. 2016. Protection of Big Data Privacy. IEEE Access, 2169-3536, Volume 4, Digital Object Identifier 10.1109/ACCESS.2016.2558446.

Milchman, A., Fang, N. 2018. Prescriptive Analytics: A Short Introduction to Counterintuitive Intelligence. CreateSpace Independent Publishing Platform, 2018, ISBN: 197992970X, 9781979929707.

Minu, M.S., Ahmad, Z. 2020. Augmented Analytics: The Future of Business Intelligence. ManTech Publications, Recent Trends in Computer Science and Software Technology Volume 5 Issue 1, DOI: http://doi.org/10.5281/zenodo.3757837.

Mishra, N. 2020. International Trade Law Meets Data Ethics: A Brave New World. New York University Journal of International Law and Politics (Vol 53:2, pages 305-74), ANU College of Law Research Paper No. 21.15.

Mosavi, N.S., Santos, M.F. 2020. How Prescriptive Analytics Influences Decision Making in Precision Medicine. Procedia Computer Science. Volume 177, 2020, Pages 528-533. https://doi.org/10.1016/j.procs.2020.10.073.

Moreira, João Mendes, André C. P. L. F. de Carvalho, and Tomáš Horváth. 2019. A General Introduction to Data Analytics. John Wiley & Sons, Inc.

Muehlhoff, R. 2021. Predictive privacy: towards an applied ethics of data analytics. Ethics and Information Technology. DOI: https://doi.org/10.1007/s10676-021-09606-x.

Mukhopadhyay, N. 2000. Probability and Statistical Inference. Marcel Dekker, Inc., Volume 162. ISBN 0-8247-0379-0.

Muller, H., Freytag, J.-C.. (2003). Problems, Methods, and Challenges in Comprehensive Data Cleansing. Journal of Computer Science, Humboldt-Univ. zu Berlin, 2005, pp. 21.

Namjoshi, J., Rawat, M. 2022. Role of smart manufacturing in industry 4.0. Materials Today, Volume 63, 2022, Pages 475-478. DOI: https://doi.org/10.1016/j.matpr.2022.03.620.

Nanda, P., Kumar, V. 2022. Information Processing and Data Analytics for Decision Making: A Journey From Traditional to Modern Approaches. Information Resources Management Journal, Volume 35, Issue 2. DOI: 10.4018/IRMJ.291693.

National Cooperative Highway Research Program (NCHRP). 2003. Report 512: Accelerated Pavement Testing: Data Guidelines. National Academies of Sciences, Engineering, and Medicine. Washington, DC: The National Academies Press. https://doi.org/10.17226/21958.

Obradovic, Z. 2023. Big Data. LiebertPub. Volume 11, No.3, June 2023. ISSN: 2167-6461.

Ojokoh, B.A., Samuel, O.W., Omisore, O.M., Sarumi, O.A., Idowu, P.A., Chimusa, E.R., Darwish, A., Adekoya, A.F., Katsriku, F. 2020. Big data, analytics and artificial intelligence for sustainability. Scientific African, Volume 9, September 2020, e00551, https://doi.org/10.1016/j.sciaf.2020.e00551 .

O'Toole, T. 2020. What's the Best Approach to Data Analytics? Harvard Business Review. URL: https://hbr.org/2020/03/whats-the-best-approach-to-data-analytics .

Pajkovic, N. 2022. Algorithms and taste-making: Exposing the Netflix Recommender System's operational logics. Convergence: The International Journal of Research into New Media Technologies, Vol. 28(1) 214–235. DOI: 10.1177/13548565211014464.

Pan, D. 2015. Advanced Data Analysis: From Excel PivotTables to Microsoft Access. Proceedings of the Charleston Library Conference. DOI: http://dx.doi.org/10.5703/1288284315592 .

Petousis-Harris, H. 2020. Assessing the safety of COVID-19 vaccines: a primer. Drug Safety. (2020) 43:1205–10. doi: 10.1007/s40264-020-01002-6.

Petrescu, M., Krishen, A.S. 2018. Analyzing the analytics: data privacy concerns. Springer Link, Journal of Marketing Analytics 6, 41–43 (2018). https://doi.org/10.1057/s41270-018-0034-x .

Plato. Stanford.Edu. 2020. Scientific Research and Big Data. Stanford Encyclopedia of Philosophy. URL: https://plato.stanford.edu/entries/science-big-data/ .

Plester, V., Huylebrouck, H. 1999. The Ishango Artefact: The Missing Base12 Link. Forma, 14, 1999, pp. 339–346.

Pompeii, L.A. 1998. Inferential and advanced analysis of research data. AAOHN Journal., 1998 Oct;46(10):514-6.

Poornima, S., Pushpalatha, M. 2020. A survey on various applications of prescriptive analytics. International Journal of Intelligent Networks, Volume 1, 2020, Pages 76-84.

Pottle, J. 2021. 1000 Words: Science: Build Knowledge, Vocabulary, and Literacy Skills (Vocabulary Builders). Dorling Kindersley Limited.

Pramod, B., Shadaab, K., Vineet, K. 2021. Big Data and Business Analytics Market Report. Global Opportunity Analysis and Industry Forecast, 2021–2030. Allied Market Research, Report Code: A05903. URL: https://www.alliedmarketresearch.com/big-data-and-business-analytics-market .

Prayaga, V. 2020. Smart Diapers. Research proposal. Research Gate, DOI: 10.13140/ RG.2.2.29246.92480.

Rahm, E., Do, H.H. 2000. Data Cleaning: Problems and Current Approaches. Bulletin of the IEEE Computer Society Technical Committee on Data Engineering.

Ramageri, B.M. 2010. Data Mining Techniques and Applications. Indian Journal of Computer Science and Engineering, Vol. 1, No.4, 301-305.

Rawat, R., Yadav, R. 2021. Big Data: Big Data Analysis, Issues and Challenges and Technologies. v 2021 IOP Conf. Ser.: Mater. Sci. Eng. 1022 012014.

Razmetaeva, Y. 2020. The Right to Be Forgotten in the European Perspective. TalTech Journal of European Studies 10(1): 58-76. DOI:10.1515/bjes-2020-0004.

Ren, X., Li, X., Ren, K., Song, J., Xu, Z., Deng, K., Wang, X. 2021. Deep Learning-Based Weather Prediction: A Survey. Elsevier Journal of Big Data Research, Volume 23, 15 February 2021, 100178, https://doi.org/10.1016/j.bdr.2020.100178 .

Resnick, P., Varian, H. 1997. Recommender systems. Commun.ACM30(3):56-58.

Ridzuan, F., Zainon, W.M.N.W. 2019. A Review on Data Cleansing Methods for Big Data. Procedia Computer Science 161 (2019) 731-738. 10.1016/j.procs.2019.11.177.

Rimal, Y. (2020). Regression Analysis of Large Research Data: Dimensional Reduction Techniques. In: Dawn, S., Balas, V., Esposito, A., Gope, S. (eds) Intelligent Techniques and Applications in Science and Technology. ICIMSAT 2019. Learning and Analytics in Intelligent Systems, vol 12. Springer, Cham. https://doi.org/10.1007/978-3-030-42363-6_35 .

Ropke, S. 2005. Heuristic and exact algorithms for vehicle routing problems. Ph.D Thesis, Department of Computer Science at the University of Copenhagen (DIKU). Available at: https://www.researchgate.net/publication/200622125_Heuristic_and_exact_algorithms_for_vehicle_routing_problems.

Roy, D., Srivastava, R., Jat, M. & Karaca, M.S. 2022. A Complete Overview of Analytics Techniques: Descriptive, Predictive, and Prescriptive. Decision Intelligence Analytics and the Implementation of Strategic Business Management. EAI/Springer Innovations in Communication and Computing. Springer, Cham. https://doi.org/10.1007/978-3-030-82763-2_2 .

Sadiku, M.N.O., Shadare, A.E., Musa, S.M., Akujuobo, C.M. 2016. Data Visualization. International Journal of Engineering Research and Advanced Technologies (IJERAT), Volume 02, Issue 12, December 2016. ISSN: 2454-6135.

Salgador, J.P.Z. 2018. Data Analytics with Tableau: The Trend Lines Models. SSRN Electronic Journal, DOI:10.2139/ssrn.3282727.

Saltz, J., Dewar, N. 2019. Data science ethical considerations: a systematic literature review and proposed project framework. Springer Link, Journal of Ethics and Information Technology, 21, pages 197–208 (2019), DOI: https://doi.org/10.1007/s10676-019-09502-5 .

Sarker, I.H. 2021. Data Science and Analytics: An Overview from Data-Driven Smart Computing, Decision-Making and Applications Perspective. SN COMPUT. SCI. 2, 377 (2021). https://doi.org/10.1007/s42979-021-00765-8 .

Sarpong, K.A-M., Arthur, J.K. 2013. Analysis of Data Cleansing Approaches regarding Dirty Data – A Comparative Study. International Journal of Computer Applications (0975 – 8887), Volume 76– No.7, August 2013.

Sarstedt, M., Mooi, E. 2014. A Concise Guide to Market Research. Springer. DOI: 10.1007/978-3-642-53965-7. ISBN: 978-3-642-53964-0.

Sayantan Khanra, Amandeep Dhir, A. K. M. Najmul Islam & Matti Mäntymäki. 2020. Big data analytics in healthcare: a systematic literature review. Enterprise Information Systems, 14:7, 878-912, DOI: 10.1080/17517575.2020.1812005.

Scales, J.A. 1998. What is noise? Geophysics, Vol. 63, No.4 (July-August 1998), p. 1122-1124.

Sharma, S., Deepmala, Upadhyay, A.K. 2021. Information Literacy: An Overview. Ilkogretim Online - Elementary Education Online, 2021; Vol 20 (Issue 1): pp. 4227-4234. doi: 10.17051/ilkonline.2021.01.465

Sheik A. A., Selvakumar, S., Ramya, C. 2017. Descriptive Analytics. Volume: Applying Predictive Analytics Within the Service Sector. IGI Global book series Advances in Business Information Systems and Analytics (ABISA). ISSN: 2327-3275; eISSN: 2327-3283.

Shoaib, G., Nandi, S. 2022. Power Bi Dashboard for Data Analysis. International Research Journal of Engineering and Technology (IRJET), Volume 09, Issue 07. e-ISSN: 2395-0056.

Siegel, E. 2013. Predictive Analytics: The Power to Predict Who Will Click, Buy, Lie or Die. John Wiley & Sons, Inc. ISBN: 978-1-118-35685-2.

Singh, N. 2020. Hypothesis Testing in Data Science. The School of Computer Applications, Babu Banarasi Das University. DOI: 10.13140/RG.2.2.29097.62560.

Singh, M., Lilo Jnr, R., Ghutla, B., Aessaan. 2017. M. Walmart's Sales Data Analysis - A Big Data Analytics Perspective. In Proceedings of The Conference: 2017 4th Asia-Pacific World Congress on Computer Science and Engineering (APWC on CSE). DOI:10.1109/APWConCSE.2017.00028.

Sivarajah, U., Kamal, M.M., Irani, Z. and Weerakkody, V. 2017. Critical analysis of Big Data challenges and analytical methods. Journal of Business Research, Volume 70, January 2017, Pages 263-286.

Skiera, B., Miller, K., Jin, Y. 2022. The impact of the General Data Protection Regulation (GDPR) on the online advertising market. Bernd Skiera; 2022.

Someh, I., Davern, M., Breidbach, C. F., & Shanks, G. 2019. Ethical Issues in Big Data Analytics: A Stakeholder Perspective. Communications of the Association for Information Systems, 44. https://doi.org/10.17705/1CAIS.04434.

Srinivasa, K., Kurni, M. (2021). Tools for Learning Analytics. In: A Beginner's Guide to Learning Analytics. Advances in Analytics for Learning and Teaching. Springer, Cham. https://doi.org/10.1007/978-3-030-70258-8_5.

Stanford Edu. 2020. Scientific Research and Big Data. Stanford Encyclopedia of Philosophy. URL: https://plato.stanford.edu/entries/science-big-data/ .

Stewart, M. 2019. Handling Big Datasets for Machine Learning. Towards Data Science. URL: https://towardsdatascience.com/machine-learning-with-big-data-86bcb39f2f0b.

Stobierski, Tim. 2021. A Beginner's Guide to Value-based Strategy. Harvard Business School Online. 5 January. Accessed May 23, 2023. https://online.hbs.edu/blog/post/data-analytics-vs-data-science .

Stoudt, S., Vásquez, V.N., Martinez, C.C. 2021. Principles for data analysis workflows. PLoS Comput Biol 17(3): e1008770. https://doi.org/10.1371/journal.pcbi.1008770 .

Su, S., Du, L. 2021. Learning from the past: development of safe and effective COVID-19 vaccines. Nat Rev Microbiol. 19:211–9. doi: 10.1038/s41579-020-00462-y.

Taherdoost, H. 2020. Different Types of Data Analysis; Data Analysis Methods and Techniques in Research Projects. International Journal of Academic Research in Management (IJARM), Vol. 9, No. 1, 2020, Page: 1-9, ISSN: 2296-1747 © Helvetic Editions LTD, Switzerland.

Taherdoost, H. 2021. Handbook on Research Skills: The Essential Step-By-Step Guide on How to Do a Research Project. Amazon Kindle.

Teh, H.Y., Kempa-Liehr, A.W., Wang, K.I.-K. 2020. Sensor data quality: a systematic review. Journal of Big Data, (2020) 7:11. DOI: https://doi.org/10.1186/s40537-020-0285-1.

Thanekar, S.A., Subrahmanyam, K., Bagwan, A.B. 2016. Big Data and MapReduce Challenges, Opportunities and Trends. International Journal of Electrical and Computer Engineering (IJECE), Vol. 6, No. 6, December 2016, pp. 2911–2919, ISSN: 2088-8708, DOI: 10.11591/ijece.v6i6.10555.

Tsyen, N., Chan, T. 2016. Defining and Conceptualizing Actionable Insight: A Conceptual Framework for Decision-centric Analytics. Conference Proceedings of the Australasian Conference on Information Systems.

Udechukwu, A., Ezeife, C., Barker, K. 2003. Independent De-duplication in Data Cleaning. Conference Proceedings for the 5th International Conference on Enterprise Information Systems (ICEIS) 2003.

University of Pennsylvania. 2022. 5 key reasons why data analytics is important to business. 20 October. Accessed May 20, 2023. https://lpsonline.sas.upenn.edu/features/5-key-reasons-why-data-analytics-important-business.

Vachharajani, B. and Pandya, D. 2022. Dimension reduction techniques: Current status and perspectives. Proceedings to the International Conference on Additive Manufacturing and Advanced Materials (AM2). Volume 62, Part 13, pages 6913-7340 (2022).

Van der Broeck, J., Herbst, A.J., Cunningham, S.A. 2005. Data Cleaning: Detecting, Diagnosing, and Editing Data Abnormalities. PLoS Medicine, Volume 2, Issue 10, DOI: 10.1371/journal.pmed.0020267.

Van Es, K. 2022. Netflix & Big Data: The Strategic Ambivalence of an Entertainment Company. Sage Pub Journals, Journal of Television & New Media, DOI: 10.1177/15274764221125745.

Wang, J.ames. 2021. The Importance of Data Analytics in Today's Business World. Australian National Institute of Management and Commerce. 23 July. Accessed May 22, 2023. https://www.imc.edu.au/news-archive/the-importance-of-data-analytics-in-today-s-business-world.

Wang, L., Alexander, C.A. 2016. Machine Learning in Big Data. International Journal of Mathematical, Engineering and Management Sciences, Vol. 1, No. 2, 52–61, 2016 ISSN: 2455-7749.

Wickham, H. 2014. Tidy data. Journal of Statistical Software 14(10), DOI: 10.18637/jss.v059.i10 .

Williams, B.K., Brown, E.D. 2019. Sampling and analysis frameworks for inference in ecology. Wiley Online Library, Methods Ecol Evol. 2019;10:1832–1842. DOI: 10.1111/2041-210X.13279.

Wise, J. 2021. Covid-19: Rare immune response may cause clots after AstraZeneca vaccine. BMJ 2021; 373 doi: https://doi.org/10.1136/bmj.n954.

Wratten, L., Wilm, A. & Göke, J. 2021. Reproducible, scalable, and shareable analysis pipelines with bioinformatics workflow managers. Nat Methods 18, 1161–1168 (2021). https://doi.org/10.1038/s41592-021-01254-9 .

Xu, Z., Shi, Y. 2016. Exploring Big Data Analysis: Fundamental Scientific Problems. Ann. Data. Sci. 2, 363–372 (2015). https://doi.org/10.1007/s40745-015-0063-7 .

Xu, K., Li, Y., Liu, C., Liu, X., Hao, X., Gao, J., Maropoulos, P.G. 2020. Advanced Data Collection and Analysis in Data-Driven Manufacturing Process. Chinese Journal of Mechanical Engineering (2020) 33:43. DOI: https://doi.org/10.1186/s10033-020-00459-x.

Yaseen, H.K., Obaid, A.M. 2020. Big Data: Definition, Architecture & Applications. International Journal on Informatics Visualization. Vol.4 (2020), No.1, e-ISSN : 2549-9904, ISSN : 2549-9610.

Yenni, G.M., Christensen, E.M., Bledsoe, E.K., Supp, S.R., Diaz, R.M., White, E.P., et al. 2019. Developing a modern data workflow for regularly updated data. PLoS Biol 17(1): e3000125. https://doi.org/10.1371/journal.pbio.3000125 .

Yesuf, E.A. et al. 2022. Self-reported side effects of the Oxford AstraZeneca COVID-19 vaccine among healthcare workers in Ethiopia, Africa: A cross-sectional study. Public Health, 19 July 2022, Sec. Infectious Diseases, Surveillance, Prevention and Treatment, Volume 10 - 2022 | https://doi.org/10.3389/fpubh.2022.937794.